Valued or Forgotten?

Independent Visitors and disabled young people

Abigail Knight

SUPPORTED BY

JOSEPH
ROWNTREE
FOUNDATION

NATIONAL
CHILDREN'S
BUREAU

The National Children's Bureau (NCB) works to identify and promote the well-being and interests of all children and young people across every aspect of their lives.

It encourages professionals and policy makers to see the needs of the whole child and emphasises the importance of multidisciplinary, cross-agency partnerships. The NCB has adopted and works within the UN Convention on the Rights of the Child.

It collects and disseminates information about children and promotes good practice in children's services through research, policy and practice development, membership, publications, conferences, training and an extensive library and information service.

Several Councils and Fora are based at the NCB and contribute significantly to the breadth of its influence. It also works in partnership with Children in Scotland and Children in Wales and other voluntary organisations concerned for children and their families.

Contents

Acknowledgements

The results of this research project would not exist if it had not been for the enthusiastic participation of all the children and young people, their foster carers, keyworkers and Independent Visitors, who agreed to take part in the study. Everyone was so kind and keen to help, often providing me with food and drink as well as transporting me to and from stations. Confidentiality and anonymity have, of course, been promised so I am unable to name any of them, but my thanks, in the first instance must go to them.

My thanks also go to all the Independent Visitor Scheme Coordinators who answered my questions and spent time contacting potential participants. I would particularly like to thank Jean Clark, Jan Goudge, Jenny Parkes, Karen Matthews, Jeanette Everton, Terry Murphy and Helen Peters.

I am very grateful for the support, advice and encouragement given to me by the project's two Advisory Groups, the first (main) advisory group was made up of:

Dr Priscilla Alderson	University of London
Claire Benjamin	Joseph Rowntree Foundation
Professor David Berridge	University of Luton
Jean Clark	Independent Visitor Scheme Co-ordinator, Leeds
Mike Evans	National Institute for Social Work
Vivien Freeman	Westminster Social Services
Dr Chris Hanvey	John Ellerman Foundation
Ann Macfarlane	Independent Research and Training Consultant
Veronica Plowden	The Children's Society
Christine Sturrock	Independent Visitor, Leeds
Dr Linda Ward	Joseph Rowntree Foundation and the Norah Fry Research Centre

and the second group consisted of young people from the Manor Gardens Disabled Young Person's Group: Danny Batten, Joe Finlay, Sarah Charles, Kelly Niven and Lorraine Mullen.

My thanks must also go to the National Institute for Social Work, in particular the Director, Daphne Statham, for supporting the research and for adminstering the funding.

Finally, the research and this report would not have been possible without the financial support of the Joseph Rowntree Foundation. I would like to acknowledge not only the Foundation's generosity in funding the project, but also for having the confidence in a freelance researcher such as myself to undertake the study. I hope they will see that it has been a valuable and worthwhile piece of work.

Abigail Knight
April 1997

Introduction

In the run-up to the 1997 General Election, the Leader of the Labour Party, Tony Blair MP, announced that all children and young people in residential homes would have an Independent Visitor under a Labour Government (Brindle, 1997). The proposal indicates a growing concern for children experiencing abuse whilst in the care of the local authority and especially those in residential care.

Yet why is it recommended that young people have Independent Visitors, rather then say, more social work support or counselling? This publication seeks to answer this question in reporting the findings of a piece of research on Independent Visitors and disabled children and young people, which took place between May 1996 and April 1997. The study was funded by the Joseph Rowntree Foundation and supported by the National Institute for Social Work.

The idea for the research came out of a conference on Independent Visitors held in London in May 1995, which was organised by the Thomas Coram Foundation, *Community Care* magazine and the National Institute for Social Work. The conference showed that although the appointment of an Independent Visitor for a child or young person who is being looked after but has little or no contact with his or her parents, is a legal duty under the Children Act 1989, only a handful of local authorities were actually using them. Where Independent Visitors *were* being used with great success, many of the children and young people who were benefiting were physically and/or learning disabled.

It was felt, therefore, that the use and role of the Independent Visitor needed to be examined and publicised. It could be argued, as evidence cited in Chapter 1 shows, that looked after disabled children are the most vulnerable and often forgotten group of young people in the country. The appointment of an Independent Visitor, it was hypothesised, could potentially be extremely valuable for them. The title of the report, then, is a recognition of two points: one, it appears that both disabled children, who are looked after, and Independent Visitors have largely been forgotten; and two, both disabled young people and Independent Visitors should be valued to a much greater extent. It was felt that this situation needed exploring more thoroughly.

The main aim of the research, of which this report is the result, was to investigate and, thereby, raise the profile of the Independent Visitor. Within this overall aim, the project sought to find out how many Independent Visitor schemes were running in England and Wales, how these were being organised and to discover how many disabled children and young people had access to an Independent Visitor. The main focus of the research study was then to explore the effects the appointment of an Independent Visitor had had on 20 disabled children and young people, and to see whether these relationships had been beneficial to them. The project aimed to find out if the Independent Visitors had contributed to the disabled young people having a better quality of life, and whether their existence had helped the young people's voices and needs being heard and met.

The research aims touch upon a number of issues which will be examined in Chapter 1 by way of background: the Independent Visitor as outlined in the Children Act 1989, children's rights, and the situation for disabled children living away from home.

In order to carry out the research, contact was made with all the schemes that were known to exist before the end of 1996. Interviews were conducted first with over 20 Independent Visitor Scheme Coordinators. Observations and interviews were then undertaken with 20 disabled young people in foster and residential placements across the country, their foster carers or keyworker and their Independent Visitors. An explanation of the choice of research methods and a discussion of the ethical issues involved is given in the Appendices.

Chapter 2 reports the results of the survey undertaken with the Independent Visitor Scheme Coordinators. It explores the issues faced by schemes as well as demonstrating how schemes have tended to be organised and how many children and young people – disabled and non-disabled – they are serving. Chapter 3 presents the views, including some non-verbal responses, of the young people who took part in the research. To protect their identity, all names, and sometimes genders and ages, have been changed.

The Independent Visitors interviewed in the research and their views on why they applied, the training, assessment and support they received, are introduced in Chapter 4. Chapter 5 is an examination in detail of some of the main themes and benefits of Independent Visitors which came out of the interviews. The important issue of advocacy is explored in Chapter 6. Chapter 7 outlines some of the main difficulties faced by Independent Visitors in undertaking the role. The report concludes with messages from young people and their Independent Visitors, a summary of the findings, and some recommendations for an improved service.

A word about terminology. First, it is important, at this stage, to clarify the definition of disability which was used in this piece of research. After a long discussion with the main Advisory Group, it was agreed to include children and young people who had a physical impairment or learning difficulty, which, in line with the Children Act 1989, was permanent and substantial. It was also agreed that a child or young person who had a behavioural or emotional problem would only be included if these difficulties were accompanied by a physical or learning disability.

Second, there has been much debate about whether it is correct to say 'child with a disability' or 'disabled child'. The former, many argue, emphasises the fact that the child is a child first and foremost and has a disability second. Others argue that children and adults who have impairments are disabled by the way that society is organised, in that physical and social barriers which exist prevent these people from participating fully and from having the same opportunities as others. This argument emphasises disability as a social construction and therefore says that it is important to call these children and adults, 'disabled'. It is beyond the scope of this report to look at these arguments in any depth. Although there are important messages in both these terms, the latter is mainly used in the text.

Finally, it is necessary to point out that the research was undertaken in England and Wales, rather than anywhere else in the United Kingdom, because the Children Act 1989, which makes provision for Independent Visitors, only covers these two areas.

1. Independent Visitors and disabled children: an overview

It is remarkable that, despite a wealth of written material on children's rights (Franklin, 1995; Dalrymple and Hough, 1995; Cloke and Davies, 1995, for example) and declarations that the 1990s should be seen as the decade of the recognition of children's rights (Hamilton, 1996), so little has been produced relating to the role of the Independent Visitor. In fact, apart from the very recent proposal announced by Tony Blair, referred to in the Introduction, Independent Visitors rarely get even a mention in books and articles. Independent Visitors have been discussed by only a handful of authors, most of whom are referred to below, and in two articles written by Mel Swales (1992, 1993), Development Officer for Children's Services in Leeds, a social services department which is running the largest and one of the earliest schemes to be established.

Independent Visitors appear in only one piece of previous research, *Capitalising on the Act* (HMSO, 1992), which looks at the implementation of the Children Act 1989 in London. That research showed that only three volunteers had, at that time, actually been approved in the whole of London, with four more in the process of approval.

Despite the Children Act 1989 now being in its sixth year, the debate about the Independent Visitor and its role is, therefore, still in its infancy. Some of the issues relevant to the debate are outlined below so the research findings can be put in some kind of meaningful context.

Who are Independent Visitors?

Under the Children Act 1989, local authorities are required to appoint Independent Visitors for children and young people who are looked after by the local authority and who have either not been visited by a parent or someone with parental responsibility in the previous year, or where communication between such a person and the child or young person has been infrequent (Children Act 1989, Schedule 2, Section 17(1)).

Independent Visitors are volunteers, are entitled to expenses and are recruited, assessed, trained and approved by or on behalf of the local authority. Both the Children Act 1989 (Schedule 2, Section 17 (1b)) and the *Children Act Guidance and Regulations, Volumes 3 and 4* (Department of Health, 1991) emphasise that the visitor must be an 'independent' person. This is, in fact, where the term 'Independent Visitor' originates as the Children Act does not actually use the name. This 'independence' means that the visitor must not be an elected or co-opted member or a paid officer of the social services department or the partner of any of these. If the child is accommodated in a voluntary or private organisation, the visitor must not be a member, patron or trustee of this organisation.

Independent Visitors have the duty of 'visiting, advising and befriending the child' (Section 17(2)). The Children Act Guidance stresses that it will depend on the qualifications, experiences and wishes of the volunteer and on the circumstances and views of the young person what sort of role the Independent Visitor, in practice, takes on. What the guidelines are more clear about is that whatever the volunteer does 'should be directed at contributing to the welfare of the child' (Department of Health, 1991). This may include encouraging the young person to 'exercise his rights and participate in decisions' affecting him or her, listening to and advising the child and attending review meetings. In 'exceptional circumstances', it may be appropriate for the young person to spend some time at the Independent Visitor's home or even have an overnight stay. The guidelines clearly point out that whatever the Independent Visitor does, the volunteer must not be used as a substitute for professional services such as counselling or skilled advocacy if the child or young person needs them.

All these points will be discussed again in more detail in an examination of the young people and the Independent Visitors who participated in this study.

How many disabled children are eligible for an Independent Visitor?

There are three problems in estimating how many disabled children are eligible for an Independent Visitor. The first is that there is a dearth of accurate figures relating to disabled children living away from home, simply because they have just not been recorded. One reason for this is that when social services departments record, for the Department of Health, the number of children they have looked after in any one year, they are not required to break down the figure into categories which would include disabled children and young people. The second is that there is a difference between the number of children who live away from home on a long-term basis and those who are seen as 'looked after' by the local authority under Section 20 of the Children Act 1989, which sets out the circumstances in which children should be accommodated. The third is that there are no official figures on how many children and young people, who are looked after, have little or no contact with their parents. As Morris (1995) has said,

> methods of recording and measuring therefore obscure disabled children's experience once again.

In analysing the OPCS survey of 1988, Loughran, Parker and Gordon (1992) estimated that children with disabilities are eight times more likely to be in the care of local authorities than non-disabled children, derived from the figure that 28 per cent of children in the care of local authorities were disabled. The difficulty with this estimate, however, for the purpose of this research, is that Loughran, Parker and Gordon included in their figures children with emotional and behavioural difficulties.

In regard to the number of children who are looked after and do not have contact with their parents, Loughran, Parker and Gordon, estimate that a third of the disabled children in the OPCS study 'could be regarded as being isolated from their parents'. In addition, an increase in 52-week residential placements may even push up this figure.

So how many disabled children living away from home fit the criteria for having an Independent Visitor? According to the *Statistical Bulletin 1996: Children Looked After by Local Authorities* (Department of Health, 1996) there were 49,000 children looked after under Section 20 of the Children Act 1989 at the end of March 1995. Using Loughran, Parker and

Gordon's figure that 28 per cent of children in the care of the local authority are disabled, it can be concluded that there could be about 14,000 disabled children and young people who are looked after. Using Loughran, Parker and Gordon's figure that about a third of these are isolated from their families, it is estimated that there could be about 4,500 disabled children and young people in the country, including those with emotional and behavioural difficulties, who might be eligible for an Independent Visitor.

Why are Independent Visitors important for disabled children?

It is hard to deny the view that disabled children are among the most vulnerable in the public care system (Russell, 1995). Not only are these children disabled, many may have limited communication skills and extra care needs, making abuse and/or neglect more likely. They also may live away from their families, often far away from their place of origin, with the result that their contact with their families and other significant adults is restricted. Both Marchant and Page (1993) and Westcott (1993), in their work on child protection and disabled children, have emphasised the 'double jeopardy' of disabled children living away from home. As Morris (1995) concludes, in her research and policy review of disabled children living away from their families,

> disabled children experience patterns of care which would never be tolerated for non-disabled children.

The appointment of an Independent Visitor could be vital, then, in safeguarding the rights of disabled children living away from home and could go some way in redressing their particular vulnerability. This point, which is the crux of this research study, has been recognised by several authors. Morris (1995) asks if disabled children living away from home are having access to an Independent Visitor and Russell (1995) recommends that 'more attention should be paid to the possibility of appointing an independent visitor'. Loughran, Parker and Gordon (1992) state that 'the contribution of local-authority appointed independent visitors should be especially important' for 'isolated' disabled children.

Independent Visitors and children's rights

Advocacy

In its report *Services to Disabled Children and their Families*, the Social Services Inspectorate (1994) recommended that:

> Social services departments should consider the introduction of an advocacy scheme for disabled children to enable them to express their wishes and feelings.

Because Independent Visitors are expected, according to the guidelines, to help young people exercise their rights and participate in decisions, the role of the Visitor has been likened to that of an advocate. Hough (1995), for example, has called the Independent Visitor a 'watered-down version of a Citizen Advocate'. Hough goes on to say that:

> local authorities committed to a children's rights perspective need to encourage and enable Independent Visitors to take on advocacy roles for young people with whom they are matched.

As the findings of this project unfold, it can be seen that there are both parallels and differences between Independent Visitors and advocates. This issue is discussed in more detail in Chapter 6.

Complaints

The Children Act 1989 also places a duty on local authorities to set up a complaints procedure (Section 26). Supporting a disabled child or young person in making a complaint may potentially be another role for an Independent Visitor. Sir William Utting in his review of residential care (Utting, 1991) makes a direct link between Independent Visitors, complaints and disabled children and is worth quoting in full:

> it may be hard for a child with disabilities to obtain effective access to a complaints procedure. Using telephone helplines may be difficult because of problems with oral communication and the limitations on privacy imposed by severe immobility. I consider therefore that consideration should be given, in light of the operation of the new complaints procedure, to extending the appointment of independent visitors to children with disabilities. Such visitors, who would need appropriate communication skills, would play a particular role in relation to protection from abuse and access to representation and complaints procedures.

Sir William Utting's words are noteworthy for two reasons: first, he clearly gives the Independent Visitor an advocacy role; second, he says that Independent Visitors should be *extended* to disabled children, implying an assumption that the provision in the Children Act is only for non-disabled children, another illustration of the disabled child often being devalued or even forgotten.

2. Independent Visitor Schemes: the situation in 1996

The following findings were collated from 23 Independent Visitor Schemes in England and Wales, during the period May to November 1996. Further details about the methods used are given in the Appendices.

History and management of schemes

The Independent Visitor Schemes included in the survey developed between 1991 and 1996, with the majority being set up in 1993 and 1995.

At the time of the survey, 12 schemes were run by social services departments, in a variety of settings, ranging from the Child Protection Unit, to Adolescent Services and the Inspection Unit. Eleven of the schemes were run by voluntary agencies, who received funding from social services departments. Voluntary agencies who were running Independent Visitor Schemes included NCH Action for Children, NSPCC and Spurgeon's Child Care.

Independence

When asked what they thought the main advantages and disadvantages were of the scheme being placed in either social services or a voluntary agency, the most common reply included a discussion around independence. In fact, only two Coordinators who were interviewed did *not* mention the issue. Those whose schemes were placed in social services felt that the scheme lacked independence, in that they were inextricably linked to the local authority and were perceived to be so by young people, whilst for those in voluntary agencies, their independence from social services was perceived to be the main advantage. Those in social services who found this independence less of a problem were the schemes based either in the department's Inspection Unit or completely separate from any other section in social services.

Funding

One of the main problems faced by schemes based in voluntary agencies was the use of service level agreements and the need to secure funding from year to year, a process which caused much uncertainty for both Coordinators and Independent Visitors. This also caused difficulties for some Independent Visitors in obtaining money for travel and expenses, which is reported in Chapter 7.

The relationship between schemes and social services

Many Coordinators based in voluntary agencies felt that they were not taken seriously enough by the social services department and consequently, did not always receive referrals or adequate information from social workers. Many had spent much time attending team meetings to publicise the scheme and felt they needed to dispel doubts and fears. One scheme even produced a video to show to social services professionals in the hope this would increase the number of referrals.

Some Coordinators, mainly in voluntary agencies, felt that many social workers were wary of the scheme and were possibly threatened by the role of the Independent Visitor, because they perceived it as being about children's rights. Furthermore, some Coordinators felt that many social workers were ambivalent towards and even jealous of the role of the Independent Visitor, as they wanted to take the young person out themselves but did not have the time. One Coordinator said that the reason why there were no disabled children matched with an Independent Visitor in that area was because the social workers she had spoken to felt that they were already doing the job of an advocate. This view assumes that the role of the Independent Visitor is only about advocacy and forgets about the significance of independence.

Coordinators based in social services departments felt that one of the main advantages of being based in the department was that the scheme had a higher profile and as a consequence, they had a closer relationship with social work staff. However, two Coordinators based in social services felt

that some social workers were expecting too much of Independent Visitors in their referrals, wanting the volunteers to take on specific, professional and sometimes quite specialist roles, such as therapeutic tasks, to help young people come to terms with abuse or their racial identity, for example.

In addition, the majority of the Coordinators based in social services (8 out of 12), were expected to run the Independent Visitor Scheme as part of another role, such as a Children's Rights Officer or a Reviewing Officer, meaning that they had, in many cases, only a few hours a week to do the job. Coordinators based in voluntary agencies were more likely to be employed on a full time or part time basis solely to run an Independent Visitor Scheme.

How many?

Schemes

There were about 23 schemes running in 1996 with a few more developing in early 1997 and a few local authorities using Independent Visitors on an ad hoc, case-by-case basis. As a rough estimate, the number of local authorities using Independent Visitors is unlikely to be more than 40. Given that there were, before the establishment of unitary authorities when the survey took place, in the region of 120 local authorities in England and Wales, this means that only about 33 per cent of local authorites were using Independent Visitors, despite the fact they all have a legal duty to do so.

The survey undertaken showed that the majority of schemes were set up in the North of England, with two schemes in Wales, a handful of schemes in the South East and the Midlands and only one scheme in the whole of the South West.

Independent Visitors and young people (disabled and non-disabled)

The survey of schemes showed that, by the end of 1996, there were approximately 370 Independent Visitors recruited in England and Wales.

Of these 370 Independent Visitors only 235 were actually matched and visiting a child or young person at the time of the survey, a result of a lack of referrals or the need to make careful matches. Given that there were about 49,000 looked after children and young people in 1995 (Department of Health, 1996) and that social services departments, such as the Leeds Independent Visitor Scheme, for example, estimate that about 10–15 per cent are isolated from their families, about 6,000 children (non-disabled *and* disabled) are probably eligible for an Independent Visitor. A tiny proportion, about 4 per cent of children and young people are, therefore, receiving a service to which they are entitled.

Tables 2.1, 2.2, 2.3 give a breakdown of the number of children and young people who were matched with an Independent Visitor, in the categories of type of placement, age and race.

Table 2.1:   Percentage of children and young people who were matched with an Independent Visitor (by Placement) (N = 235)

Placement	Percentage
Foster care	47
Residential care	38
Other (residential school, after care)	15

Table 2.2:   Number of children and young people who were matched with an Independent Visitor (by Age) (N = 235)

Age	Number
Under 5	1
5–10	29
11–15	148
16 and over	57

It is interesting to note that the majority, 63 per cent, of young people with an Independent Visitor were in their early- to mid-teens. This is, perhaps, an indication that for many young people in the care system, these years are the most difficult in terms of being isolated from families and unsettled in placements.

Table 2.3: Children and young people from a black or minority ethnic group who were matched with an Independent Visitor (N = 235)

Number	Percentage
50	21

The proportion of young people with an Independent Visitor from a black or minority ethnic background was quite high. This is a reflection of two points: first, the fact that there is a higher proportion of children from mixed parentage groups who are looked after, and second, that unaccompanied refugee young people fit neatly into the criteria for having an Independent Visitor, in that they are looked after but have little or no contact with their parents. There are already two schemes running, both in London, which have been set up solely to provide Independent Visitors for refugees.

Disabled children and young people

The survey showed that 32 of the 235 children and young people matched with an Independent Visitor were disabled, nearly 14 per cent of the total, with 17 disabled children waiting to be matched. Using the estimate that there are about 4,500 disabled children and young people who are eligible for an Independent Visitor, as discussed in Chapter 1, no more than 1 per cent of disabled young people are receiving a service to which they are entitled under the Children Act 1989.

Table 2.4: Disabled young people with an Independent Visitor (by Age) (N = 32)

Age	Number
Under 5	0
5–10	4
11–15	9
16 and over	19

Although this was a very small sample, the ages of disabled young people with an Independent Visitor (see Table 2.4) contrasted with those who were non-disabled. With the disabled group, the majority were over 16, rather than in their early- to mid-teens, as reflected in the ages of the disabled young people who participated in the study. This finding is, perhaps, an indication that disabled young people are more likely to become looked after and/or isolated from their families in their later teens, although it is not possible to make concrete conclusions from such a small sample.

Table 2.5:   Disabled young people with an Independent Visitor (by Placement) (N = 32)

Age	Number	Percentage
Foster care	13	41
Residential care	11	34
Other		
Adult hostels	4	13
Residential school	2	6
Independent living	1	3
Supported accommodation	1	3

Table 2.6:   Disabled young people from a black or minority ethnic group who were matched with an Independent Visitor (N = 32)

Background	Number
Black African	1
Mixed parentage	1

At the time of the survey, out of the 32 disabled children with an Independent Visitor, one was black African and one was from a mixed parentage background (Table 2.6). Of the 17 disabled children waiting to be matched, two of these were from African-Caribbean families, whilst one was from a mixed, Asian and white, background. The black African young person, who had an Independent Visitor, participated in the research.

The findings relating to non-disabled and disabled children presented above showed that over 21 per cent of the children who had an Independent Visitor were from a black or minority ethnic group. The figures relating to disabled children, however, showed that only 6 per cent of disabled children with an Independent Visitor were from a black or minority ethnic background. This illustrates one of two points, which cannot be answered categorically here: either there are fewer black/minority ethnic *and* disabled children, who are being looked after and have little or no contact with their parents, than white and disabled children, or that these children are not being referred for an Independent Visitor and are, therefore, missing out on a service to an even greater extent than their white counterparts.

Recruitment of Independent Visitors

Advertising

All the Scheme Coordinators had used a variety of methods to advertise for potential volunteers to be Independent Visitors. These included the following:

- distributing leaflets and posters around public buildings and shops in the local area;
- forging close links with the local Volunteer Bureau;
- using contacts at a local children's forum, made up of people from the statutory and voluntary agencies, to advertise the need for volunteers;
- placing an advertisement in the local paper;
- writing an article about the scheme for the local paper;
- using adverts and interviews on local radio;
- working closely with local community groups, and in particular, groups representing people from different minority ethnic groups;
- contacting local colleges and universities, asking for mature students in particular;
- advertising in the local government newsletter;
- advertising in parish magazines;
- using the volunteer section in Wednesday's *Guardian*;
- by word of mouth.

Most Coordinators had experienced periods when responses to different methods were very poor and others when they were very busy with applications. One Coordinator reported having just organised a large recruitment drive, involving the local radio and distributing flyers in county council buildings, but had received only one response. Another had held several open evenings in order to give members of the public information, but again had not been successful. Coordinators reported that by far the most successful way of recruiting volunteers was by using the local press, whether this involved placing adverts or writing press releases or articles. This seemed to attract a steady trickle of applicants.

With one exception, none of the Coordinators had a different recruitment procedure for Independent Visitors for disabled children. Instead, they asked prospective volunteers, during the assessment, whether they would be happy to be matched with a disabled young person. Because one Coordinator had a number of disabled children waiting to be matched, she intended advertising for people who would be particularly interested in being matched with a disabled young person.

Type of volunteers

Many Coordinators reported difficulties in recruiting men and volunteers from black and minority ethnic groups. Although the need to recruit volunteers from minority ethnic backgrounds has been successfully addressed by some family based respite care schemes (Poonia and Ward, 1990), problems in attracting volunteers from such groups was found in recent research undertaken by the National Centre for Volunteering (1996). The study concluded that the image and culture of volunteering was perceived as a predominately white, middle class activity. It found that young people (under 25), older people (over 55), unemployed people and disabled people are also under represented as volunteers.

Some of the Scheme Coordinators included in this survey had taken proactive steps to recruit people from black and minority ethnic backgrounds. The most common way was by forging close links with local community groups, but this had not always been very successful. One very effective way, which certainly worked for one scheme, was to write an article for the local paper about Independent Visitors, mentioning that the scheme particularly needed African-Caribbean volunteers, which provoked a good response.

The vast majority of Independent Visitors, according to the Coordinators interviewed, are white women. Yet their ages and backgrounds, in terms of type of education, employment, class and whether or not they have had previous experience of working with children and young people, including having their own, varied considerably. This is reflected in the brief descriptions of the Independent Visitors who participated in the research, presented in Chapter 4.

In order to attract more men, one scheme wanted to mention the shortage and their need for more male volunteers, again in an article in a local paper. It was felt, however, that the risk of attracting paedophiles was too great so it was not pursued. One volunteer project, which recruits advocates for people with severe learning difficulties, found that they attracted more men when the advertisment mentioned the issue of people's rights (Rickford, 1996).

Although two of the Independent Visitors who participated in the research were disabled, none of the Coordinators interviewed had taken proactive steps to recruit disabled volunteers.

Assessment and vetting

All the schemes had a thorough assessment and vetting process, involving a series of stages, not always in the same order, and included the following:

- application form
- assessment undertaken by the Coordinator at a home visit
- induction/training course
- a formal interview with a panel
- police checks
- references.

The need for such a long and detailed assessment and vetting procedure is clearly crucial when approving members of the public to have contact with vulnerable children and young people. This key issue will be discussed in more detail in Chapter 7.

Training and supporting Independent Visitors

Most schemes expected prospective volunteers to attend a series of training sessions as part of the assessment. The length of these varied considerably from two evenings to seven full days, with the average being about six two-hour evening sessions. Topics covered include child protection issues, how social services works, the Children Act 1989, confidentiality and advocacy. Few of the schemes offered specific training sessions on disability, although some issues were covered as part of another section, usually the one on equal opportunities.

Training after approval tended, for most schemes, to be offered on an ad hoc basis, as part of a support group, which usually met about every six weeks. Topics covered were identified by the volunteers themselves and include drug and HIV awareness, living in residential care, loss and separation and more on child protection issues, such as sexual abuse. Again, disability issues – such as communication skills, and working with children with challenging behaviour – did not have a high profile, which caused some problems for some Independent Visitors, as further chapters illustrate.

In regard to support, all the schemes ran a group for Independent Visitors, with meetings varying in frequency, most being about every six weeks. All the Coordinators offered support on an individual basis, either on the telephone or in person. Some carried out home visits to volunteers on a regular basis to monitor how things were going, whilst the majority offered support if and when it was necessary. Two of the schemes had a newsletter for Independent Visitors and organised outings for the volunteers and their young people, about twice a year.

As part of the survey, Scheme Coordinators were asked for their views on the role of the Independent Visitor, and on the issue of advocacy, in particular. A discussion of these views – and the views of others on these issues – will be presented in Chapters 5 and 6.

3. 'Someone to talk to': young people's views about Independent Visitors

Introducing the young people

The 20 young people who took part in the research were all aged between 13 and 24, with the majority being in their late teens. It was not the intention of the research to focus on this age group, but reflects the fact that most young people who have an Independent Visitor are in the older age group. Two of the young people who participated were over 21 and were, therefore, not officially eligible for Independent Visitors, because they no longer came under children's services. For these young people, their Independent Visitors chose to continue in the role as they felt a long-term commitment to the young person.

Out of the sample of 20, 12 were young women and eight were young men. Nineteen were from a white British background, and one was black African, reflecting the proportion of white and black/minority ethnic disabled young people in Britain with an Independent Visitor, as shown in Chapter 2. Of the 20 young people, seven were in foster care, 11 in residential care, one was in a residential school and one was living independently.

The group of young people who participated had a wide range of abilities and disabilities, including four who did not communicate through speech and had severe learning difficulties, two who used wheelchairs, while the rest had some degree of learning disability, sometimes combined with an emotional or behavioural difficulty. The vast majority were attending either a special or mainstream school or college, with two attending a day centre and two in full time employment, one in a hairdressers and one in a factory.

The length of time that the young people had had an Independent Visitor varied considerably. One young person had had one for a few weeks, whereas others had been seeing the same person for over four years with the average being about a year. Five of the young people already knew the person in another capacity, such as a social worker, residential worker or parent of a school friend, before they became their Independent Visitor.

The young people had been referred for an Independent Visitor, in most cases, by their social worker at a review meeting. Only one of the young people had asked for an Independent Visitor; she had known about Independent Visitors because another girl in the foster home already had one. None of the other 19 young people knew what Independent Visitors were or what they did before it was suggested to them by their social worker. The young people had been referred to have an Independent Visitor because their family contact had either ceased or was very limited and because the young people, it was felt, needed new experiences and relationships outside their foster or residential placement.

Almost all the young people were seeing their Independent Visitor on a weekly or fortnightly basis. With one exception, all the Independent Visitors took the young person out so they could do things together away from the placement. The most common activities included going to the cinema, going for a meal, swimming, bowling, horse-riding, roller or ice-skating and shopping. For nine of the young people, going to the Independent Visitor's home on an occasional or regular basis was an important part of the relationship. The activities undertaken and the possibility of the young person going to the Independent Visitor's home brought up important issues for the Visitors and are examined further in subsequent chapters.

Initial reactions

Many of the young people who participated in the study felt the need for more information about Independent Visitors and their role, before or certainly at the time that the suggestion of having one was made. Three of the young people said clearly that they had not been sure about having an Independent Visitor, despite the fact that two of these had received leaflets, explaining their role:

'I wasn't sure what an Independent Visitor did.'

'I didn't know what to think at the time.'

Others were much clearer and more positive at the prospect, from the very beginning:

'It sounded great – it was someone else to talk to.'

Although none of the young people who participated in the research had been involved in the selection of their Independent Visitor, many of them had requested a particular kind of person. Most of the girls had specifically requested a woman, while two of the boys wanted a male Independent Visitor. Some of the young people emphasised qualities that would help them talk to the Independent Visitor:

'I wanted to have an older person so I could to talk to them.'

'She had to be understanding.'

For the young people who had never met the prospective Independent Visitor, meeting them with the Coordinator was the first and very important part of the matching process:

'I met her and looked at her and thought, yes, I've got a nice person. I think it'll work out OK.'

Non-verbal responses and reactions

Because they could not be interviewed using any form of verbal communication, four of the 20 young people were observed with their Independent Visitors. Three of these young people all reacted very positively when their Visitors arrived to see them. They were visibly excited, clapping their hands, laughing, smiling, making sounds and gestures to collect their coat in order to go out. These ways of expressing pleasure were continued when the young person and the Independent Visitor went out, whether it was to the park or for a walk. Although the other young person was certainly not negative when seeing the Independent Visitor, she did not show the same degree of interest and pleasure at spending time with the person. It later transpired that the Independent Visitor was not able to visit the young person on a very regular basis and saw his role as more about liaising with staff than taking the young person out.

Friends to go out with and talk to

All the 16 young people who were interviewed were very positive about their Independent Visitors. The comments expressed were all related to one of two things: having someone to go out with and/or having someone else to talk to. When asked to describe their Independent Visitor, the most common response was that he or she was a friend:

> 'She takes me out in the car. We get some bread for the ducks. I like her. She's a nice lady, she's a nice friend.'

> 'She's somebody I can talk to. She's a friend so if I have any problems, I can go to her.'

Similarly, when asked if they thought the Independent Visitor had helped them and if so, how, the young people spoke again about having someone to confide in and about going out:

> 'I go out with friends more now, so I'm more independent.'

> 'I think he does help me because it's nice to have another friend to go out with. It's nice to have someone to take you out.'

> 'It's nice to have an Independent Visitor, to have someone there when you need to talk.'

> 'She's helped me to come out of my shell.'

> 'It's fun to go out with someone because most friends you don't see at weekends.'

One young person felt strongly that she should have had an Independent Visitor years ago so that there could have been someone to confide in:

> 'If I'd had an Independent Visitor a couple of years ago, I think some of the things in my life would have been easier. I was in trouble when I was about 12 and I didn't have anyone to talk to at the time. Nobody knew about it until I was 16. If I'd had someone at the time like an Independent Visitor, I would've been able to say something.'

Helping when there is no family contact

About half of the young people who participated in the study had some form of limited (often supervised and/or infrequent) family contact. Of those who did not have any family at all, two of them compared themselves to other young people in care who knew something about their families and their past, and spoke forcefully about the importance of having an Independent Visitor to bridge this gap.

One of these young persons had known his Independent Visitors (two Visitors) for several years, during which time he had moved placement many times. The Visitors could offer continuity for him, which no one else could, crucial for his sense of identity:

> 'They know my past. They remember things I don't know. They bring memories up, then I know more.'

The other young person spoke at length about her experiences in residential care and how having an Independent Visitor had helped her feel less lonely:

> 'It was nice to think that you have a person who belongs to you type thing. When you live in a residential home, you get a lot of children who have family contact. At the time, I didn't and I used to think, they have someone to go to, why can't I?'

> 'I was really envious of the others and that, because they had family contact and went out. I was really lonely 'cos I didn't have anyone. So many staff come in and out of your life and it's really, really unsettling. I used to hate living in a place like this. You make ties with someone and then they've got to go, it really does your head in. You feel so lonely and you don't want to get close to anyone because they'll only leave.'

Having an Independent Visitor had made a difference to this young person:

> 'I felt happier, I had something to look forward to and it kept my mind more positive you know. I'd get really excited because Helen [the Independent Visitor] was coming.'

Another young person, who visited the Independent Visitor at home sometimes, thoroughly enjoyed mixing with the Visitor's young grandchildren, who called him their cousin or uncle. Another young person called her Independent Visitor auntie, especially when other young people at the residential unit were around, to show them she had some family.

A relationship to choose

Children and young people who are looked after, and particularly those who are disabled, have, as the young person above said, numerous people, mainly professionals, coming in and out of their lives. For the vast majority of these young people, there is no sense of choice or control over these relationships, whether to have them at all, or when and where to see them.

As explained in Chapter 1, the Children Act 1989 emphasises the need for children and young people to make their own decisions over whether to have an Independent Visitor, if the authority is satisfied that the young person has sufficient understanding (Schedule 2, Section 17(5)). This choice is crucial in allowing this relationship to be one of a different nature from that with professionals, probably the reason why most of the young people described their Independent Visitors as friends.

Having the choice to end the relationship is also an important part of having a sense of control, which so many children and young people who are looked after lack in their lives. One of the young people who participated in the study had made a decision to stop seeing his Independent Visitor because he felt he no longer needed the relationship. When asked what he felt about this, he answered:

> 'I feel OK about it because it was my choice. It was nice in the sense that I left the relationship; it wasn't someone leaving me.'

Reviews

Twelve of the young people who participated in the research were able to talk about their review meetings (when the young person, family and professionals meet to talk about the placement and plans for the child's care, usually held every six months). Two of the young people had not had reviews since being matched with their Independent Visitors. Of the other ten young people, *all* felt they had benefited from having their Independent Visitors present at their review meetings. They all felt more supported and less alone in the meetings:

> 'He's on my side.'

'I felt more comfortable because I wasn't on my own. I wish he'd been there when I first came into care. I was right nervous.'

'It's someone there if you get stuck with something.'

'It's helpful because she's my friend and I'm not alone.'

Many of the young people felt helped by their Independent Visitor talking on their behalf in review meetings:

'He comes to all my meetings and if I need help saying things, he'll say it.'

'Sometimes I tell him to tell everyone at the meeting what I think.'

'They can put things across.'

Talking about problems and making complaints

Although the young people placed a lot of emphasis on being able to talk generally to their Independent Visitors very much as friends, when it came to more serious matters like discussing specific problems or making a complaint, most of the young people said they would turn to other people for help, usually their carer, keyworker or social worker. One young person said that his Independent Visitor 'isn't trained' to deal with his problems and another said that 'I talk to a member of staff if I can'.

However, for two of the young people, talking to their Independent Visitors about problems was crucial in the absence of anyone else:

'I did tell her [the Independent Visitor] about here [the residential unit], that they were giving me a hard time, because she understands. The social worker is busy and isn't there when you need her.'

'I couldn't talk to the staff. It was more private talking to John [the Independent Visitor].'

When it came to making a complaint, six out of 12 of the young people who were able to talk about this issue said that they would turn to their social worker for advice, three said they would turn to their carer or keyworker, while three said they would ask their Independent Visitor.

When Independent Visitors did not help

Only one young person identified any problems in having an Independent Visitor. Although the young person was very positive about her Visitor, she commented that the Independent Visitor sometimes 'tried too hard and came across as motherly'.

The same young person, who used a wheelchair, felt offended on a few occasions whilst out shopping with her Independent Visitor when shop assistants spoke to the Independent Visitor over her head – a common experience for many disabled people. The young person concerned did not feel that she could speak to the Independent Visitor about this and felt that more training on this and other disability awareness issues should be given.

Independence

Some of the young people spoke about the importance of the Independent Visitor being someone outside social services:

> 'When you live in residential care and you have a social worker and all that, sometimes it's nice to have someone in your life who's totally independent, who's not from your social worker's side of things or your family, someone you can just meet . . .'

> 'In my situation, it involved social services. It was a personal thing. I wanted to tell someone outside, not inside, because then there would've been more trouble, more hassle. If there'd been an outsider, it would have been easier to talk.'

Two of the young people felt that if Independent Visitors were appointed by social services directly, they would have to write reports on them, making the relationship more formal:

> 'When you're in care, there's enough paperwork on you anyway, you can do without it.'

For many of the young people, however, whether or not the Independent Visitor was recruited by social services was just not important. What mattered more was that the volunteer was someone the young person could talk to easily.

4. Constant people: the Independent Visitors

What sort of people?

The 20 young people who took part in the research were matched with 15 women, three men and two couples. All the volunteers were from white British backgrounds. Both findings reflect previous research into volunteering (National Centre for Volunteering, 1996), as outlined in Chapter 3.

Sixty per cent of the volunteers were in the 40 to 60 age group, with most of these being in their 50s. Three volunteers were in their 20s, three in their 30s, whilst the two couples were in the 60 to 70 age group. The distribution of ages reflects the fact that many of the Independent Visitors felt that they were able to commit themselves to the young people, as they had already established their careers and/or their own families, more likely for those in their 40s and 50s.

With regard to employment, the volunteers came from a very wide range of backgrounds. They included three administrators, a picture editor, a teacher, a social worker, a shop assistant, a nurse, a classroom assistant, two residential workers and three foster carers. Two of the women did not work as they had family commitments, one of the men had recently been unemployed and both the couples were retired.

Whilst the vast majority had experience of working with children and young people, either as a parent or in employment, only five of them had direct experiences of disabled children and young people. These people were either parents of a disabled child or had worked with disabled young people as a nurse or in residential work. Two Independent Visitors, each from the couples referred to above, were disabled themselves.

How did the volunteers first hear about Independent Visitors?

Ten (50 per cent) of the volunteers learnt about Independent Visitors from either an advert or an article in their local paper. Five (25 per cent) already knew the young person in another capacity. One person saw a poster in the library, another went to the local Volunteer Bureau, one read about a scheme in the council newsletter and two approached the social services department directly to see if any children needed volunteer befrienders. One of these people had heard a child saying on a bus that he wished he had grandparents, whilst the other had two disabled children of her own and wished to offer her help.

Why did they apply?

All the volunteers came across as people who wanted to help others in a general sense, as they felt they had some time to spare and appropriate skills. One person admitted that she felt better about herself if she was involved in voluntary work, whilst another said that he felt it might help his career prospects.

Many of the volunteers felt concerned about children and young people and felt that, because they had had a happy childhood, they wanted to give something back:

> 'I feel childhood is really important and that if you have a good childhood it does set you up and hopefully you'll be a decent citizen. I think it's awful when things go so terribly wrong and there's no one there to back you up. Children in care haven't got anyone to fall back on.'

Some of the volunteers felt especially concerned about looked after young people and felt they could help them:

> 'It's a tough world isn't it? I think you need somebody. I think some teenagers, anyway, don't think they're loved very much and those in a home particularly need somebody who is theirs, so you don't have to share them.'

One Independent Visitor spoke about her wish to help disabled children in particular:

> 'I felt strongly that so many children are abandoned just because they are disabled, not because they've done anything.'

Commitment

Most of the Independent Visitors said they were attracted to the role because it involved a long-term, one-to-one relationship. This need to be committed to the role, a requirement made by schemes, should not, therefore, be viewed as restrictive, as for many of the volunteers, this was the main reason for applying in the first place.

> 'It's something you can't just pick up and drop. It's one-to-one and I like that idea.'

> 'When I started the training, I knew that it was going to be a total commitment for me. You're committed to a child, which is terribly important – you can't let them down. They've been let down too many times.'

> 'I wanted to be someone who wouldn't let her down.'

These views were also reflected in the Independent Visitors' relationships with the young people: one volunteer who started working for social services and had to stop being an Independent Visitor continued to see the young person on a voluntary basis, without receiving expenses, another person had become the young person's respite carer and was looking into fostering him full time, whilst two had continued in the role despite the young people no longer coming under children's services. One of these two volunteers commented:

> 'I won't leave him now. I don't want to leave him. It's like having a friend.'

Many of the volunteers said they would continue seeing the young person as long as the young person wanted it, regardless of their age:

> 'I'll carry on as long as she needs me . . .'

> 'If for some reason I didn't see her, I'd worry about her forever. It's good to form a relationship and a bond.'

> 'I'm not going to dump her, it's not on . . .'

Training, assessment and support

All but one of the 20 Independent Visitors were very positive about the training they received as part of the assessment process. Some felt the training had been very long but was necessary as there was so much to learn. No one felt put off by the length of time the training, assessment and matching took, which, on average, was about six months. On the contrary, many felt that the long process made them realise that they really did want to be an Independent Visitor and that the training was an important preparation for the role:

> 'The training was like having a baby. It was a needed time before you actually got your child. In those months that you were waiting, you're preparing and getting the idea that you are eventually going to have a child. However impatient you are, it won't bring that time any earlier and if it is earlier it won't be to your good.'

The one Independent Visitor who was quite critical of the training had attended a training course of only two evenings. She felt that it was too short and did not equip volunteers for the role, something she still felt unclear about when she took part in the research. Some of the volunteers felt a bit frightened by the information they received on the course, which related to the sort of problems the children might have or the sort of situations in which they might find themselves. However, they agreed that it was necessary and did not, in the end, put them off:

> 'It was horrific!'

> 'A lot of things that came to light made it feel a bit scary'.

The most positive comments about the training related to the opportunity of meeting other volunteers:

> 'The course was lovely. It was really good, very interesting. We made friends with other Independent Visitors. It's been like a social club.'

All but one of the volunteers felt supported in the role of Independent Visitor. The 19 who felt supported had access to the Coordinator whenever they needed, either in person or on the telephone. Regular (every 6 to 8 weeks) support groups were held so that volunteers could meet others and share ideas and problems. The one Independent Visitor who did not feel supported thought the scheme she was linked to needed to have more support groups and other events at which ideas and difficulties could be discussed. Another Independent Visitor wanted to see more events – perhaps twice a year –

when all the volunteers and young people could meet together, as she, at times, felt the role could be isolating.

None of the Independent Visitors who participated in the study had received extra training because they were linked with a disabled young person. Although some commented on the danger of professionalising the role of the Independent Visitor by giving a lot of training, most felt that they could do with more training on disability issues. One Independent Visitor, who was matched with a severely learning disabled young person felt unsure of what she was doing and wanted more training:

> 'I feel a bit out of my depth. I don't feel I know enough about it. I don't know what's expected of me or what I could do to help more. No one in the group knows enough about it. I do need more training.'

Others also wanted more training on disability issues; on topics such as different conditions of disability, autism for example, and on what to expect, how to deal with fits and with challenging behaviour:

> 'I think there would be more people perhaps willing to take on a disabled child if there was more training provided. The training was more geared towards "normal" kids.'

> 'With disabled children, you need a certain amount of knowledge about what you're dealing with.'

The Independent Visitors who took part in the research all spoke at length about how they saw their role, how they felt the young person had been helped, and any problems they had encountered. These issues will be now be examined in the next three chapters.

5. Broadening horizons: the role of the Independent Visitor in the lives of disabled young people

A special friend

Chapter 3 showed how the young people who took part in the study felt that the Independent Visitor was first and foremost a friend who was someone they could go out with and talk to. This view was echoed by the vast majority of Independent Visitors, Scheme Coordinators, foster carers and residential workers who were interviewed:

'My role is to be a friend, to listen and have fun, to laugh.' (Independent Visitor)

'The role is to provide consistent visiting, friendship and support.' (Scheme Coordinator)

'Frances is like a friend to Jenny, a special person for her.' (Foster carer)

'She's a friend, a companion, a buddy.' (Residential worker)

> *Example 1* One young person, Emily who is 17, goes out regularly with her Independent Visitor, usually for a meal or to the pictures and they once went to 'Top of the Pops' at the BBC. Emily, who described her Independent Visitor as 'like a sister and a friend' was also able to talk to her about her feelings when she was going through a difficult court case involving contact with her siblings.

A different perspective

Part of this friendship role, it was felt by most of the participants, was to broaden the horizons of young people who, because they were disabled and accommodated, were in danger of seeing little outside a life of professionals and outings arranged by their keyworker or foster carer:

> 'Anything that involves the children having a social life outside here, in the big wide world, must be good for them. They don't have many friends who they bring home. Many children in care vegetate and become institutionalised.' (Residential worker)

> 'It's a good idea because it gives them another outlook on life, outside the family.' (Foster carer)

> 'My role is to broaden her horizons. I can take her to places she doesn't go to. I can give her a different angle on life.' (Independent Visitor)

Building confidence

Linked to broadening the horizons of disabled young people was the job of helping to build up the young person's confidence, commonly identified by Independent Visitors as part of their role:

> 'My role is to help John be as positive as he can about himself and that takes all kinds of shapes.'

> 'She needs to have her confidence built up, she needs new experiences. If I can open up a new world for her, then I'm doing her good.'

Example 2 One Independent Visitor had introduced the young person to painting, as it was a hobby of hers. The young person, who had a learning difficulty and lacked self-confidence, had never painted before and discovered that she was very talented; this was a real boost to her self-esteem.

Another way of giving the young person more confidence, identified by Independent Visitors, was by allowing the young person to choose the activity that they would do together and encouraging the young person to stand by the decision:

> I don't like to tell her what we would do. She's got to make up her own mind – that's one of the things, to encourage her to speak for herself.'

Independence

Some of the participants spoke about the Independent Visitor's independence and how important it was for the young person that the role was different from that of the social worker:

> 'There's got to be an establishment part for Mike [young person] and we're the back-up to the establishment. We want to be as non-establishment as possible. He's had enough establishment to last him the rest of his life.' (Independent Visitor)

> 'The social worker knows an awful lot about what's good for him, although she doesn't probably spend the time that I'm able to – it's a different sort of time, it's an organisational time.' (Independent Visitor)

> 'She needed someone else as a friend, completely independent of anybody with officialdom.' (Foster carer)

For the participants who spoke about independence as a significant issue, no distinction was made between those Independent Visitors recruited by social services and those who were recruited by a voluntary agency. What was more important was that the Independent Visitor is not paid:

> 'If he was on the payroll, he'd have a vested interest. But he's not and because it's on a voluntary basis, his motivation has got to be different.' (Residential worker)

Doing ordinary things

For many disabled young people in the care system, it is often not possible to have ordinary experiences. Going to the park or to the shops regularly might be avoided by carers or residential workers because of lack of time and resources, access problems or concerns about potential behaviour difficulties with some young people with severe learning disabilities. Going to someone's house for tea or staying the night cannot be done spontaneously because of the need for social services and police checks to be carried out, which can take several weeks and sometimes months.

Although the same checks are made on Independent Visitors and their families, these are carried out well before the Independent Visitor is approved and matched with the young person. Going for tea or staying the night on an occasional basis can then be done without too much planning.

Example 3 Erica is 14, on a full care order and has only limited, supervised contact with her family. Apart from school and occasional outings with her foster carers, her main social outlet is a local youth club, which is run by social services. One of the most important aspects of her relationship with the Independent Visitor is going to her house for Sunday lunch on a regular basis. Her foster carer spoke at length about the benefits this had brought Erica.

'It's so good because everything else has been things like the family centre, or with supervision, or somebody official always being there. With Kate being an Independent Visitor, there's no strings attached. It's like Erica acquiring older friends.'

'Erica comes back delighted. In school they'll say, "Oh, we went to Granny and so-and-so", but children like Erica can't say that . . . it's good for her morale to say, "I've been out with Kate". It's a boost.'

Example 4 Steven is 15 and lives in a residential unit. When he made friends with another boy at school, the boy's parents asked the school if Steven could come home for tea. Social services were contacted who advised that the best way of proceeding was for them to become Steven's Independent Visitors. Now Steven sees his school friend and his Independent Visitors about every fortnight, when they go to a local youth club and have a fish and chip supper at home together.

Steven's keyworker at the residential home was very positive about the relationship:

'It works with Jim and Maureen because they know they don't have to go over the top with him . . . it's the ordinary things that count. It wouldn't matter if they just took him for tea – that's a special thing to him.'

Experiencing family life

It is inevitable that all children and young people who are looked after, have experienced some disruption in their family life. Many have been abandoned or mistreated and have ended up either in someone else's family or in a residential setting with little or no contact with their relatives. As shown in Chapter 1, disabled children and young people are even more likely to have these kinds of experiences.

Like some of the young people whose views are expressed in Chapter 3, many of the Independent Visitors, foster carers and residential workers felt that having an Independent Visitor had enabled the young people to experience an 'ordinary' family:

> 'She's learning about a real family. It's good for her to know there are families who stay together and can laugh and joke and tease each other.' (Independent Visitor)

> 'You can get so institutionalised in a place like this – there's a big world out there. The more contact they can have and see how families work and function the better. We take for granted our families. You think the children know but they don't.' (Residential worker)

Example 5 Liz is 15, has lived in a residential unit for five years and has no contact with her family. Because she has autism, severe learning disabilities and challenging behaviour, the possibility of moving to a family placement had been discounted by the social services department. Vivien, Liz's Independent Visitor, has been having her home to tea once a fortnight for about six months. Liz has enjoyed mixing with the Independent Visitor's three daughters and has not displayed any difficult behaviour.

As a result, social services are now looking into the possibility of finding a family placement for Liz. Vivien has been able to contribute a lot of useful information to the planning meetings, including a written report on Liz's visits to her home, so that the planning for Liz's future is carried out as carefully as possible.

Helping out in crisis situations

Two of the Independent Visitors were able to help the young people when their foster carers found themselves in crisis situations. One young person spent Christmas Day with his Independent Visitor, as one of his foster carers was seriously ill in hospital, and another spent the night at her Independent

Visitor's home when her foster carer suffered the bereavement of a close relative.

These examples illustrate again how Independent Visitors are acting, first and foremost, as friends to the young people with whom they are matched. In both situations, it felt quite natural for both the young people and their foster carers to request help from the Independent Visitor in an emergency, in the same way that most people would have a friend or relative to call upon in a similar situation. The alternative, for both young people, would have necessitated social services (possibly the emergency social worker, who would not know the young person) being contacted and the young people being accommodated with strangers.

Preparing young people for leaving care

For ten (50 per cent) of the young people who participated in the research, their Independent Visitors had played an important part in preparing them for leaving care, whether this was going to a residential home for adults, semi-supervised accommodation or independent living. Independent Visitors had contributed to planning meetings and taken it upon themselves during outings and visits home, to help the young people gain important skills in shopping, dealing with money and cooking.

Above all, the Independent Visitors have been able to provide a much needed continuity for the young people, at a time of traumatic change:

> 'Debbie [the Independent Visitor] has been the one person who's been consistent from the move here to the move there and has kept up contact like a family member would.' (Residential worker)

One Independent Visitor said she was appointed solely for the purpose of being a constant figure in the young person's move. Many of the Independent Visitors who had not yet needed to be involved in the young person's preparation for leaving care felt strongly that this would be an important role:

> 'We're in for a tough time over the next two to three years and I feel I'll be there for her, and that's important.'

> 'It'll be important to see where she is, to share with her. If she was put into a bedsit, it'd be lovely to go and see it and for her

to know there's someone else at the end of the phone if there's a problem. That's what they need because they have to be independent so early and go out into the world. She'll need lots of support, lots and lots. She's not worldy-wise or street-wise.'

> *Example 6* Robert is 17 and is due to move away from his foster family within a few months. As he has a learning difficulty and low self-esteem, there are plans for him to move to semi-independent accommodation. However, he will be expected to organise his own finances. Robert's Independent Visitor has accompanied him to one of the residential units which has been suggested by his social worker and to some local banks to find out about applying for an account. She has also gone shopping with him to help him practise buying groceries and dealing with money.

One of the most complex and controversial issues relating to the role of the Independent Visitor in the lives of disabled young people is that of advocacy. This will be examined in Chapter 6.

6. Fighting for a cause: are Independent Visitors advocates or just friends?

The guidelines on Independent Visitors state that although the volunteer may become involved in helping the young person exercise his or her rights, the Independent Visitor is not a skilled advocate. Probably because this has not been defined any further, the extent to which Independent Visitors should or should not be advocates has become a controversial and unresolved issue for many Managers and Coordinators of schemes.

When asked what they thought of the advocacy issue, 20 per cent of the Coordinators who took part in the study felt that Independent Visitors are advocates, another 20 per cent said that they are definitely not advocates, with the other 60 per cent saying that they may be, depending on whether or not the volunteer wished to take on this role. One Co-ordinator likened the role of the Independent Visitor to that of a 'watered down Guardian ad Litem' (a child care professional who is appointed to safeguard the interests of a young person in legal proceedings), while another said that Independent Visitors 'were just friends'.

Definitions

Advocacy has been defined as:

> speaking up for, and supporting, a person or issue to the benefit of the individual or groups of individuals concerned. (Baxter and others, 1990)

In his study of citizen advocacy, Simons (1993) defines the concept as:

> the development of a supportive one-to-one relationship between an unpaid private citizen and someone who is vulnerable or at the risk of isolation, with the aim of offering some protection to the latter and help to achieve his or her personal goals.

Simons makes a distinction between *expressive* advocacy, which means providing friendship and emotional support, and *instrumental* advocacy, which means helping someone to achieve a goal by taking practical measures.

In considering the advocacy versus friendship role of Independent Visitors, it is also important to define the concept of friendship. Richardson and Ritchie (1990), who are quoted in Simons (1993), outline three characteristics of friendship: intimacy (including trust, loyalty, continuity and the sharing of feelings and experiences); company (going out and doing things with, or spending time at home together); and providing practical help (including advice).

When an Independent Visitor is an advocate

Reviews

Where the advocacy role of Independent Visitor seems to be most clear is in relation to review meetings. Chapter 4 has shown how the young people in the study viewed their Independent Visitors first and foremost as friends, whom they could talk to and have as supporters in meetings. The same view was held by the vast majority of Independent Visitors, 16 of whom had attended the young person's review meetings. They saw their advocacy role as speaking up for the young people in such meetings, if necessary:

> 'My role is to be her friend, to be there for her, to talk for her at her reviews if she wants me to . . .'

> 'The role is to befriend the child, to speak up for them, to put their views across at their reviews, to look at the world from the child's point of view.'

One Independent Visitor, for example, who was linked with a young person with severe learning disabilities, had learnt very quickly from getting to know the young person, that the contact she had with her father, though limited, was extremely important to her. When suggestions were made in the young person's review meeting that contact with her father should be reduced, the Independent Visitor was able to speak on behalf of the young person and managed to ensure the contact was not decreased.

Advocating when a young person moves

Only one Independent Visitor felt she was an advocate rather than a friend to the young person; she did not see the young person on a regular basis. She had played a major part in looking after the interests of the young person, who had severe learning disabilities, when she moved from one residential home to another:

> 'My assumption is that it is an advocate role. My liaison has been with the home and making sure the home is doing a good job, rather than being close to Hazel.'

Two other Independent Visitors, who saw themselves as the young person's friend rather than advocate, also took on this important role. Like the example given above, these two young people also had severe learning disabilities and no speech. Through the significant deterioration of their behaviour, they had shown that they were not happy in the home in which they were living. In both situations, the Independent Visitor initiated discussions with social services, to whom they expressed their concerns. As a result, one of the young people moved to another placement, which was much smaller and more geared towards meeting her needs.

Protecting and monitoring quality of care as a substitute parent

One of the Independent Visitors referred to above felt, as many others did, that what she was doing was what any 'good' parent would:

> 'I like to think I'm doing what his Mum would . . .'

> 'If he were mine, you know, you look at it that way, if he were mine, I'd be most unhappy . . .'

> 'If somebody's got someone around, like a parent, who questions and kicks up a fuss, social services listen.'

Two managers of residential homes, both in the private sector, felt that an important part of the Independent Visitor's role was to keep an eye on practice at the home and to ensure that the young person was being looked after as well as possible. One Independent Visitor had ensured that the young person, again someone with severe learning disabilities, had received more activities to stimulate her. The manager felt that this had benefited the young person:

'The knock-on effect is that the Independent Visitor can create different things happening here which is beneficial to Laura [the young person]. It makes us keep doing things for her – it's an incredibly important role.'

'If we're talking about the Children Act 1989, Independent Visitors and all that kind of language, it suggests something more official than a friendly auntie. I feel that the Independent Visitor's role ought to be to keep check on the private sector because my experience of it has been so negative.'

To illustrate these points, one Independent Visitor helped to improve the quality of life for one young person, with severe learning disabilities, by monitoring the care given by the residential unit and in protecting the young person's welfare. She felt concerned about the physical well-being of the young person, in that her hair had become badly out of shape, her personal hygiene had deteriorated due to an increasing weight problem and her clothes had become too tight. After speaking to the residential workers about her concerns and putting them in writing, the physical care of the young person markedly improved.

Although the study did not reveal any examples where Independent Visitors had helped expose severe maltreatment or abuse of young people, their role of visiting a residential or foster home as an independent person interested in a young person's welfare might make this possible. As Hoodless (1997) has suggested:

the presence of volunteers may also be protection for vulnerable children.

Furthermore, one Scheme Coordinator, who was interviewed as part of the research, believes that:

'Independent Visitors reduce the risk for all young people accommodated by the local authority.'

This point, however, raises issues around the need to vet and monitor closely the Independent Visitors themselves, a topic which will be addressed in the next chapter.

When Independent Visitors are not advocates

Complaints

As stated in Chapter 1, Sir William Utting has suggested that Independent Visitors should help disabled children access complaints procedures (Utting, 1991). This study, however, did not reveal any of the Independent Visitors suggesting to the young people that they make a formal complaint, despite there being possible grounds for doing so. Furthermore, the views expressed by the young people, as outlined in Chapter 3, shows that they did not tend to see Independent Visitors as people who could help them solve problems or make complaints.

Short-term problem solving versus long-term friendship

One of the residential workers felt that she had witnessed important differences between an advocate and an Independent Visitor, as the young person she was interviewed about had both. She felt that an advocate would be a paid person, often a professional, appointed for a young person for a short-term focused piece of work, whereas the role of the Independent Visitor was about taking the young person out and being their friend on a long-term basis:

> 'There was a different relationship. She [the advocate] used to work with Tom here . . . it's friends with the Independent Visitor. He sees Monica [the Independent Visitor] every week, the advocate doesn't see Tom every week, doesn't take him out every week, doesn't give him treats, doesn't have the same relationship like he does with Monica.'

Referring problems to the Coordinator

Although advocates would see their role as taking up a cause on behalf of the young person directly with the local authority, the vast majority of Scheme Coordinators who took part in the research did not expect the volunteers to take their concerns directly to the social worker or other relevant professional. Instead, they were expected to raise any worries with the Coordinator, who, in most cases, would follow up the issue. This view was echoed by the vast majority of Independent Visitors themselves.

A potential role, and the need to be flexible

Some of the Independent Visitors felt that although their main role was to be friends of the young people, they could also potentially be advocates for them if the need arose:

'If he comes and says something to us about the home that he doesn't like, that he couldn't tell anyone there, then we can put a case for him.'

The view of one residential worker was:

'I think Simon would be in a wonderful position to advocate for Paul because he now knows him very well and properly and all sides of him. He'd be in a good position to say what is in the best interests of Paul.'

The extent to which Independent Visitors are acting as advocates for disabled young people is, therefore, a very complex area. In the sense of helping a young person achieve his or her personal goals, the Independent Visitors in this research have not, in the main, acted as advocates for the young people. In the sense of speaking up for young people, however, most of the Independent Visitors in this study have been advocates during review meetings. Similarly, it can be seen that Independent Visitors are carrying out the expressive form of advocacy, as identified by Simons. When advocacy is about protecting the welfare of a vulnerable person, a major part of Simons' definition of citizen advocacy, then it is the Independent Visitors that are linked to young people with severe learning disabilities who are more likely to be taking on an advocacy role.

In the end, however, what seems to be most important for the Independent Visitors and Scheme Coordinators is the need for flexibility around the role, and for the Independent Visitor to take on whatever role he or she is comfortable with, as long as this fits in with the young person's wishes and overall welfare:

'The role is not precise. It's a role you have to play by ear to see what you need to do. You need to be as flexible as possible to do what needs to be done.' (Independent Visitor)

'It wouldn't be natural if you had to do things in a certain way.' (Independent Visitor)

Most of the Coordinators, Independent Visitors and young people, who participated in the study, were quite clear about the role of the Independent Visitor. However, the lack of clarity around the role, arising out of the need to be flexible, has caused some difficulties for both foster carers and residential workers. This is one of the problematic issues which will be examined in Chapter 7.

7. An ideal challenge: problematic issues

Reactions of foster carers and residential workers

Although the vast majority of foster carers and residential workers who took part in the research were very positive about the role of the Independent Visitor, some concerns about the lack of clarity of the role were expressed. One foster carer, who felt that there should be more written information on the role of the Independent Visitor, explained her and her husband's initial reactions:

> 'The role isn't clear. We couldn't clarify our role to theirs. Nobody said "This is what they do". We could've been suspicious. If foster carers aren't told, you can finish up with a situation where you perhaps view the Independent Visitors with suspicion and think they're there to spy on us, you can think that way.'

Similarly, one Independent Visitor said her main problem in the role was:

> 'getting the foster carers to realise you aren't spying on them.'

Several Scheme Coordinators reported incidents of foster carers putting obstacles in the way of the matching and/or outings of the young person and Independent Visitor – for example, by saying that the young person was too busy to make a convenient time to visit.

One Independent Visitor, who took part in the study, had previously been matched with an eight-year-old boy. Because the foster carers were not at all happy with an Independent Visitor being appointed, the volunteer spent over two hours explaining her role to the carers. They finally agreed for the matching to go ahead but on condition that the Independent Visitor was introduced to the boy as the foster carers' friend.

Because this would take away the role of the Visitor being the child's special friend, the Independent Visitor decided not to go ahead with the match as she felt that the relationship would start out on a deceptive basis.

Another Independent Visitor, who was interviewed for the research, had recently been matched with a disabled young woman who lived in a residential unit. The young person had a link family, whom she saw for alternate weekends. The link family had been going to foster the young person but did not because they found some of her behaviour difficult to manage. Although the Independent Visitor had been careful about making plans to see the young person on the weekend she was not going to the link family, on two occasions during a period of a few weeks she had arrived at the home only to find that the family had changed their plans and had collected the young person for the weekend after all.

Although Scheme Coordinators did not report the same problem in relation to residential homes, both the managers of two residential units, who participated in the research, felt unclear, initially, about the role of the Independent Visitor. Although they both changed their minds later and became very positive about the Independent Visitor, at first they felt they had not received enough information, which had made them feel very unsure:

'I wasn't keen on the idea at all. I didn't see the value initially.'

'I was unaware of the status of the Independent Visitor.'

And in the view of one Independent Visitor:

'The role should be clarified for staff in residential homes. I know a few people who work in residential schools or homes and I don't think they value Independent Visitors very much. There's a feeling of "Oh, they're coming to spy on us".'

One foster carer and one residential worker also reported feeling irritated at the Independent Visitor questioning the care they were giving the young person:

'A few comments have been made by the Independent Visitor where they think certain things should be done with Jane [the young person]. My answer is "You don't live with her. You don't know what she's actually like".'

'I can really appreciate the questioning, but it drives me mad at the same time.'

It is important then, that both Scheme Coordinators and Independent Visitors are aware of the potential confusions and conflicts which may arise between volunteers and others involved in the care of the young people, foster carers in particular. However, this should not detract from the fact that the young people in foster care, in this study, benefited from having an Independent Visitor as much as the young people in residential care. Furthermore, it must be said that the relationship between the Independent Visitors and foster carers/residential workers was generally found to be very good. One Independent Visitor summed it up by saying that having the foster carers' support was vital, and is something that may need to be worked on:

'I think one of the reasons for the success [of the match] is the reaction of the foster parents. Without their cooperation the whole thing would collapse. You really have to take in foster carers from the start. This is very important, as they're caring for the child.'

The need to assess and vet Independent Visitors carefully

It is now commonly known that, in most cases, the sexual abuse of children and young people is carefully planned by paedophiles (Renvoize, 1993), and any situation involving contact with young people may be exploited by them. Volunteering to be an Independent Visitor is, unfortunately, no exception to this rule, necessitating the need for a very thorough assessment and vetting procedure.

One foster carer spoke very forcefully about his fears and suspicions when an Independent Visitor was recommended for his foster son:

'When the Independent Visitor was first suggested, I was appalled at the idea. I was very suspicious of the kind of people who want to take children and teenagers out. I think it could attract strange people. You hear a lot about paedophiles. This must be the perfect job for them.'

As shown in Chapter 2, all the schemes that took part in the survey use long and detailed assessment and vetting procedures. Yet, however thorough the process is, it is, regrettably, not possible to guarantee that a paedophile will never be approved by a scheme. However, it could be argued that the process of gaining employment involving contact with children, such as unqualified residential work, for example, is a much shorter and perhaps easier one than the one prospective Independent Visitors must complete.

Claiming expenses

Three of the Independent Visitors interviewed, one foster carer and one residential worker, spoke about the difficulties in claiming expenses for taking out the young person. All were involved with schemes run by a voluntary agency, rather than directly by the local authority.

One scheme expected the young people to pay for themselves on outings, which restricted the kind of activities which could be enjoyed. One foster carer commented:

> 'Where the scheme falls down in my opinion is where the young person is expected to pay their way.'

One Independent Visitor, who had been recruited by the social services department and who had been unemployed while visiting a young person, had been able to obtain his expenses up front, to enable him to afford to take the young person out. Other Independent Visitors, however, reported waiting months to receive their expenses, and could only get money for activities for special occasions. Again, it is significant that these volunteers were recruited by voluntary organisations, indicating that many voluntary agencies are being expected to run schemes on behalf of the local authority on very small budgets.

Another difficulty some Independent Visitors faced was the need to collect receipts when paying entrance fees or for meals and drinks and so on. Some felt uncomfortable doing this in front of the young person and that it detracted from the friendship part of the role.

Restrictions on activities

In addition to feeling restricted by a lack of expenses in introducing the young person to a variety of activities, some Independent Visitors also felt restricted by the weather and darkness in the winter, living in a rural area, the scheme not being happy about the young person going to the volunteer's home, and the needs and wishes of the young person concerned.

One Independent Visitor was very anxious about taking the young person out as the young person suffered from epilepsy which was not well controlled. The Independent Visitor had had no previous experience or training in dealing with epilepsy and felt that she needed more knowledge of the condition if her involvement was to really benefit the young person.

Although the Independent Visitors recognised the importance of allowing the young people to have a choice in activities, in line with the ethos of the Children Act guidelines and in order to help build the confidence of the young people, this had sometimes caused difficulties. For example, many Independent Visitors said that the young people were choosing to go to the cinema week after week, with the result that the volunteers did not feel that they were getting to know the young people and were concerned that the young people were avoiding, probably through lack of confidence, the chance to talk. Their dilemma was to strike a balance between respecting and supporting the young person's right to choose and encouraging them to experience new things.

Although the guidelines state that the young person may visit the Independent Visitor's home 'in exceptional circumstances', going to the volunteer's home was an important part of the relationship for nine of the young people in the study. The benefits of this have already been outlined and include the opportunity to do ordinary things like going to someone's place for tea and being included in another family.

Although most schemes were happy about the young people seeing the Independent Visitor at their home, a couple of them were not. In addition, some Independent Visitors could not have the young person to their home because of travelling distances. Because they could not bring the young people home on occasions, three Independent Visitors reported feeling very restricted in what they and the young people could do together, especially during the winter months. As one Independent Visitor put it:

> 'If I could bring her home, I could do more with her. If you're supposed to be their friend, then with me, everyone comes home.'

Substituting other services

Chapter 2 reports how some Scheme Coordinators had received referrals for Independent Visitors which went beyond the remit of the role. The guidelines also state that Independent Visitors should not be expected to become involved in counselling and advising a child in complex situations, or acting as a skilled advocate.

Although 18 of the 20 Independent Visitors who took part in the research had been recruited to be a special friend to the young person as the Children Act intended, two of them had been recruited initially for other reasons. One reported being brought in by social services to provide another viewpoint in their plans to find a foster placement for the young person, and another had been appointed to fulfil an advocacy role during the young person's move. One Independent Visitor, summed this issue up by saying:

> 'We're not there for the foster parents, for social services, to do what they want or to tell tale.'

One residential worker expressed concerns that the social worker might not visit the young person as often as she should, because the young people had an Independent Visitor. Finally, although they recognised the importance of the young person having a special person, three of the foster carers interviewed also spoke about the Independent Visitor in the sense of providing respite care. One foster carer even felt that it would be nice sometime for the Independent Visitor to stay in the house with the young person while she went out shopping, another indication of the need for clear information about the Independent Visitor's role.

8. 'Spread it around the country': findings, messages and recommendations

Summary of research findings

- Despite having a legal duty to do so (under the Children Act 1989), it is estimated that only a third of the local authorities in England and Wales are appointing Independent Visitors for children and young people who are looked after and have little or no contact with their parents.
- It is estimated that only a tiny proportion, about four per cent, of children and young people who are eligible for an Independent Visitor, actually have one.
- It is estimated that only one per cent of disabled children and young people who are looked after and have little or no contact with their parents, have an Independent Visitor.
- The most effective way of recruiting volunteers to be Independent Visitors, Coordinators have found, is by placing articles and/or advertisements in the local press.
- The vast majority of Independent Visitors are white women. However, their ages, employment, experience with young people, education and class background vary considerably.
- The young people, who participated in the study, were very positive about having an Independent Visitor and clearly enjoyed the visits and outings.
- The young people who were interviewed for the research viewed their Independent Visitors as friends first and foremost, and as people they could go out with and talk to.

- Although the presence of the Independent Visitor in review meetings was greatly valued, young people did not view their Independent Visitors as people who could help them sort out their problems or make complaints.
- Disabled young people are benefiting in a variety of ways from having an Independent Visitor. These benefits include:

  - having a special friend to go out with;
  - being introduced to a broad range of activities and opportunities, which help to stimulate and build confidence;
  - having a visitor and friend outside social services and other professional groups;
  - being given the opportunity to do ordinary things, such as going to someone's house for tea;
  - experiencing family life;
  - having someone to stay with in a crisis situation, rather than having to be accommodated in a strange place;
  - being helped to prepare for leaving care, in practising skills like shopping, cooking and dealing with money;
  - having someone to support them and speak up for them, if necessary, in review meetings;
  - having someone to protect and monitor their welfare.

- The Independent Visitors who participated in the study acted as advocates in the sense of speaking up for young people, when it was necessary, in review meetings. For most of the young people, they did not act as advocates in any other sense. However, Independent Visitors are more likely to be playing the part of an advocate when they are linked to young people with severe learning disabilities.
- Although most of the Independent Visitors were extremely positive about their role, a few had experienced some problems, namely in receiving their expenses and being restricted in the sort of activities they could do with the young people.
- Some Independent Visitors and Scheme Coordinators had reported problems in their relationships with foster carers, and occasionally with residential workers, who, they felt, did not always understand the role and sometimes appeared to believe that the volunteers were spying on them.

Messages from young people

All the young people who were interviewed thought that other children and young people should have an Independent Visitor for the following reasons.

- So they could enjoy themselves:

  'Because Paula [the Independent Visitor] is great fun, a great laugh, so I think they should . . .'

  'Because they need to have a good laugh.'

- Have someone to go out with:

  'Because they get bored, unless the place has a car and can take them out.'

- Mix with a family:

  'They [Independent Visitors] are understandable and sometimes take you places if they've got the money, and they introduce you to the family . . .'

- To have a friend who is someone to talk to:

  'They're someone to talk to if you're lonely or feel you can't talk to anyone . . .'

  'It's good to have somebody else you can talk to in case you can't get on with your foster parents or whoever, just as a friend really.'

Messages from Independent Visitors

When they were asked for their overall views about Independent Visitors, all the volunteers who were interviewed were very positive about their role and the benefits it brought to young people:

'I think it would benefit a lot of other kids, especially when a lot of these disabled kids have been in care. They need to have a friend to call their own, someone just for them.'

Many of the Independent Visitors wanted to encourage other people to volunteer,

'Tell everyone to have a go.'

'I'd recommend it to anyone really, to give it a go.'

'Be one!'

but felt that there was not enough information around:

> 'I know a lot of people who'd make good Independent Visitors but don't know anything about it. There should be more publicity about it.'

> 'Spread it around the country!'

Linked to this issue of needing more information about the role of the Independent Visitor, one volunteer had a particular message for social services departments:

> 'Social services should be made aware that we're not there to tread on their toes. We are there purely as independent people who are not trying to interfere, and we might make their life easier. We must make sure that more children are aware of it.'

Should all looked after young people have an Independent Visitor?

While making concluding remarks, many of the Independent Visitors and some of the residential workers gave their views about whether all young people who are looked after, rather than just those who are without parental contact, should have an Independent Visitor.

Some very mixed views on this issue were expressed. One Independent Visitor felt that because communities were becoming less close knit, the criteria for having an Independent Visitor should be extended:

> 'It appears that there are young people that could benefit from having an Independent Visitor, who don't meet the requirements. I think if the requirements for a visitor were looked at and the funding is there, a broader spectrum of young people could have that support – I think it would be beneficial to them.'

Similarly, one residential worker commented:

> 'It would help if every young person we worked with had an Independent Visitor, definitely. They all need someone who's completely independent, who's an advocate, who they complain to, who's completely impartial.'

Others, however, had different views. Chapter 3 showed how some young people particularly valued their Independent Visitors because they did not have contact with their families like other young people in the home did. Some Independent

Visitors interviewed felt that if they were linked to young people with family contact, their role would become very complicated and sometimes difficult.

The Independent Visitors who expressed this view did not feel that they were equipped to deal with the family as well as the young person and would need a lot more training to undertake this role. Instead, one Independent Visitor felt that all children and young people who are looked after and *ask* for an Independent Visitor should have access to one.

Recommendations relating to this important issue are included below.

Recommendations for a better service

1 The criteria for having an Independent Visitor should be changed to: all children and young people who are looked after by the local authority, do not have at least monthly visits to their foster or residential home by an adult friend or an adult member of their family, and would like an Independent Visitor.

2 All local authorities in England and Wales should implement their legal duty to appoint Independent Visitors for the children and young people who meet the present criteria and the criteria recommended above.

3 The need for an Independent Visitor should be discussed in every young person's review meeting and should be part of every care plan. The role of the Independent Visitor should be clarified and established at the point of referral and during subsequent reviews.

4 The Department of Health should ensure, through regular monitoring of local authorities, that Independent Visitors are being used, as required by the Children Act 1989.

5 Local authorities should commit sufficient funding for a scheme to be run efficiently and to meet the interests of all the children and young people who are eligible for an Independent Visitor, whether the scheme is run by the social services department or on their behalf by a voluntary agency.

6 Schemes should use strict and thorough assessment and vetting procedures to ensure as far as possible the protection of all the children and young people who have an Independent Visitor.

7 Schemes should ensure that disabled young people and children from black and minority ethnic groups are being referred for an Independent Visitor, which may mean proactively seeking out referrals from specialist teams.

8 More information publicising the role of the Independent Visitor should be produced. Information, in an appropriate form, should be produced for children and young people, taking into account the learning disabilities and the specific communication needs of some young people. Information explaining the remit of the Independent Visitor, giving examples of the sorts of things they do whilst stressing the flexibility of the role, should also be produced for prospective volunteers, potential referrers, foster carers and residential workers.

9 Schemes should ensure that volunteers receive training on disability issues, including concepts of disability (such as medical model versus social model), disability equality awareness, and training and information on certain conditions, such as autism and epilepsy, and how to deal with them.

10 Schemes should ensure that Independent Visitors receive their expenses either before or shortly after the visit to the young person, in order for unemployed people and those on a low income to feel able to volunteer.

11 Schemes should proactively recruit volunteers from black and minority ethnic groups, and disabled people, by working closely with community groups and the media who represent them.

12 Local authorities and schemes should ensure that children and young people who are living a long way from their home of origin are found an Independent Visitor, who is either prepared to travel or lives in the area local to the young person's placement. Local authorities and schemes may have to set up reciprocal practical and funding arrangements with their equivalent in these areas in order to do this.

Conclusion

During the months preceding the General Election of 1997, some proposals were made to monitor the Children Act 1989 because it was feared children's rights were overriding those of adults (*The Conservative Party Manifesto*). It is ironic that one of the most enlightened measures relating to the rights of looked after young people introduced by the legislation – the Independent Visitor – has, as this research has shown, been largely forgotten.

The results of this study have demonstrated that the small group of disabled young people who have an Independent Visitor are benefiting in a considerable way. The Independent Visitors are acting as special friends to these young people and are helping to safeguard their welfare. They are reducing the isolation and loneliness many of these young people feel and are helping them to have ordinary experiences.

It is estimated that there are well over 4,000 disabled children and young people who are living away from home, isolated from their families, and with little or no contact with people outside their schools, foster or residential homes and a circle of busy professionals. By implementing the requirement under the Children Act 1989 to appoint Independent Visitors for these young people, child care professionals will be actively promoting their welfare and improving the quality of their lives.

Appendix A
Methodological issues

Survey of Independent Visitor schemes

In order to collate statistical information relating to Independent Visitors and more general information about the management of schemes, a questionnaire for Scheme Coordinators was drawn up, after consultation with the main Advisory Group. Because of the relatively small number of Coordinators in the country and because of the notoriously low level of returns of postal questionnaires, it was decided to use the questionnaire to carry out structured interviews with Coordinators.

The first task was to locate Independent Visitor Schemes in the country. This was done by contacting Jean Clark, Coordinator of the Leeds Scheme, placing an advertisement in the magazine *Community Care* and attending a forum for Independent Visitors held in Leeds in June 1996.

Between May and November 1996, the statistical and more general information reported in Chapter 2 was gathered from 23 Scheme Coordinators, using the following methods: six indepth interviews and 12 telephone interviews with Scheme Coordinators, the forum in Leeds referred to above and five postal questionnaires.

Researching the young people and their Independent Visitors: interviews and observations

In order to obtain a full picture, it was felt to be important to gather information not only from the children and young people and their Independent Visitors, but also from one other person who knew the young person well. Because all the young people were seen, for at least some of the time, in their placements, it seemed most appropriate that this person should be the foster carer or residential worker, often the keyworker.

Lists of questions to ask the young people, Independent Visitors and the foster carers or residential workers, were drawn up in consultation with the project's two Advisory Groups. Because the information required was of a qualitative, rather than a quantitative, nature, the questions were used as guidelines when talking to participants. In some interviews, particularly with the young people, some questions were not used at all, and in others, the questions were asked in a different order or with different words, to ensure that the interviews were as 'natural' as possible. For example, the term 'Independent Visitor' was not always used when talking to young people and short, simple questions, such as 'What do you do with so-and-so?' were more likely to be used than open-ended questions, such as 'What is your Independent Visitor like?'

In order to find participants for the research, a number of Coordinators were contacted. Coordinators were chosen on the basis that they were known to be running relatively large schemes in different parts of the country, and included both disabled young people and children from black and other minority ethnic groups. The Coordinators, most of whom the researcher had met in person, already knew about the research, from the forum or from the survey of schemes which was taking place.

The Coordinators contacted all the participants and social workers of the young people to ask if they would be happy taking part in the research and, if so, would they be willing for the researcher to contact them directly. None of the participants objected and, in fact, many of them were enthusiastic to take part and told both the Coordinator and the researcher that they felt strongly about the issues, and wished to take an active role.

The participants were then contacted by telephone and told more about the research. This was followed up with an Information Sheet about the research and a letter confirming the date and time of the visit. Each interview was taped, with the permission of the interviewee, in order to avoid note-taking and to enable the participants' 'voices' to be used in the findings, in the form of quotations. Only two people – one young person and one keyworker – objected to being taped. After the visits, everyone received a thank you letter or card.

From the beginning of the project, it was intended to include young people with severe learning and communication difficulties. It was clear that for these young people, it would not be possible to assess their relationship with the Independent Visitor simply by talking to them. It was, therefore, decided that it would be more appropriate to observe the young people *with* their Independent Visitor. By observing the point at which the Independent Visitor arrived or left, when visiting the young person, and some of the interactions between the two, it was felt that it would be possible to draw some conclusions on whether the relationship appeared to be important to the child and one which was valued and beneficial. Observations, like interviews, require permission from the participant, a challenging issue when working with severely learning disabled people. This and other ethical issues will now be examined.

Involving disabled children in research: ethics

Research involving disabled children presents particular challenges, especially as they belong to groups traditionally either undervalued or even ignored in the research process. Involving children (both disabled and non-disabled) in research is thankfully becoming more commonplace – a reflection of a climate, fuelled by both the Children Act 1989 and the United Nations Convention on the Rights of the Child, which recognises that children should be listened to.

Yet this increasing involvement must be accompanied by a strict adherence to certain ethical considerations so that disabled children are not used and exploited for the sake of research. Many of these issues are covered in detail by, among others, Priscilla Alderson (1995), Linda Ward (1997), Bryony Beresford (1997), Alderson and Goodey (1996). It is beyond the scope of this report to examine these issues in depth, so the most relevant points to this particular research project will now be considered.

Informed consent

In order to carry out research with children and young people, it is important to obtain consent from both parents and from the young people themselves. This consent must be an *informed* decision, based on information appropriate to the person's age and understanding.

The criteria for having an Independent Visitor is that a child or young person must be looked after by the local authority and have little or no contact with his or her parents. Because of this, it was not considered necessary to obtain permission from parents in the vast majority of cases. Where there was still involvement from parents, permission was sought from them via the residential workers or social worker.

The area of informed consent of children to participate in research is a very complex one, based on rulings arising from the Gillick judgement and the Children Act 1989, and the complicated concept of 'competence', examined in detail by Alderson (1995). As a result, the legal and ethical position of consent to treatment and research concerning children is very uncertain.

According to Beresford (1997), informed consent has three characteristics: it is based on knowledge, gained by means of understandable information; it is voluntary; and the person has the capacity or competence to give consent. It is not always easy, however, to assess whether a decision is voluntary. Children and young people, and perhaps particularly those in the care system as they often lack self-confidence, may agree to things just to please or because this is what they feel they *should* do, or simply because they are not used to being asked.

The young people who participated in the study were all sent an Information Sheet, informing them about the research, and were told about the research by a familiar person. When the researcher visited them, more information about the study was given, with the opportunity to ask questions, and the voluntary nature of participating was reinforced. Out of the 20 young people who participated, it was possible to carry out this type of negotiation with 13 of them.

For the other seven young people, who had severe learning and communication difficulties, obtaining informed consent needed particularly careful thought. Although it was not possible to give them information about the research in written form, it was possible for a familiar person to tell them about the project and that a researcher wanted to see them and their Independent Visitor. Through their own mode of communication, whether this was body language, gestures, sounds, signs and so on, it was possible for the familiar person to judge whether the young person was happy about the planned visit. In addition, on two occasions, it was possible for the researcher to see the young person a day prior to the planned visit to tell them about wanting to come and see them and their Independent Visitor. By gauging a reaction and using the views of the person who knew the young person well, such as the keyworker, it was possible to make a decision about consent and whether the visit was in the young person's best interests. On this basis, none of the young people objected to the visit.

Conducting the interviews and observations

Each interview with and observation of the young people took place at the child's foster or residential home. The young people were all given the choice of having a familiar person with them whilst the interview took place. Although this may have meant that the child's responses were sometimes inhibited, it was felt more important to give them the choice, especially if this made them feel more comfortable. Seven young people were interviewed alone.

Each interview was preceded by some general conversation to attempt to establish a rapport and by discussion about the research, what it was for and what would happen to the information. The young people (and the adult participants) were reassured about confidentiality (unless the young people disclosed information which showed they were at risk). To help put them at their ease and to feel more valued in the research process, the young people were given the opportunity to ask questions, shown the tape recorder and given the chance to listen to their own voices and to take control of it.

Giving feedback

Another important ethical consideration is the need to give feedback after the interview or observation has taken place. Each young person received a thank you card following the visit. On a couple of occasions, the young person's Independent Visitor told the researcher how much the young person had enjoyed and valued receiving the card. In addition, it is planned to produce some leaflets on Independent Visitors, in consultation with young people themselves, which will include a section on the main findings of the research project.

Valuing the disabled young person in the research process

To prevent the passive participation, and potential exploitation, of disabled children and young people in the research process, it is important to consider ways of helping them feel more valued and involved. Some useful suggestions are outlined by Ward in *Seen and Heard* (1997).

At the beginning of this project, it was hoped that the methods chosen to gather information from young people would give them the chance to talk about themselves and about a person who is there just for them, their Independent

Visitor. It was thought that by consulting the young people for their views about how the relationship had benefited them or not, they would feel valued from the start.

Furthermore, where possible, the young people were asked for their views on how Independent Visitors could be publicised and what messages and recommendations they wished to give to local authorities. It is also hoped that the leaflets mentioned previously would help the young people see some development and follow up to their initial involvement.

In the planning stages of the project, it was felt important to include disabled young people in an advisory role, a point which was discussed with members of the main Advisory Group. It was agreed that including one or two disabled young people on the main Group might be tokenistic and intimidating for the young people concerned. Instead, a disabled young people's group was contacted and members requested to help out. Five disabled young people were seen and were paid a fee for their time and expertise. They were consulted about the Questionnaires and Information Sheets for young people, early on in the study.

Limitations of the research

It is now important to outline some of the limitations of the study. First, the research is an exploratory study only. It is important, however, in that it reports the voices and direct views of disabled children themselves and shows, through numerous examples, the ways in which Independent Visitors are enriching their lives.

Second, the sample of 20 young people is small and does not claim to be representative of all disabled children and young people who are eligible for Independent Visitors, especially as the sample only included one non-white British young person. However, as Chapter 2 shows, a sample of 20 actually makes up a majority of disabled chidren and young people who presently have an Independent Visitor, so is a good representation of this small group. Furthermore, the information collated from Scheme Coordinators shows that there were, at the time of the survey, only two non-white disabled young people in England and Wales with an Independent Visitor, one of whom was included in the research.

Third, the survey of schemes only included those which existed before the end of 1996, thus excluding a small number of schemes which are starting to develop in 1997. In addition, some local authorities are known to use Independent Visitors on an ad hoc 'case-by-case' basis, volunteers who are often recruited by social workers and who are not part of a scheme or network. It is almost impossible to find out how many and which local authorities are using Independent Visitors in this way, and for this reason they have also been excluded in the research findings. Consequently, the figures, in particular, cannot be completely accurate.

Finally, because participants for the research were found through Scheme Coordinators, it was sometimes felt that the matches of young people and Independent Visitors which were working the best were the ones offered for the research, leaving aside the ones where there were problems. Difficult issues, however, were highlighted by some of the participants and these are outlined in Chapter 7, in order to balance the positive results reported in Chapters 3 to 6.

Despite these limitations, the study is a starting point in an under-researched area and uses a variety of methods which focus directly on the views and experiences of disabled young people.

Appendix B
Questionnaire for interviews with children and young people

Warm up

Introductions; general chat; explain simply and clearly purpose of research; try and gauge their understanding of their involvement and whether they have received adequate information (i.e. leaflet and/or explanation) to ensure that they have given informed consent; check they are still happy taking part; let them know how long the interview will take; reassure them there are no right or wrong answers; explain purpose of tape recorder and whether it is OK to use it; test it and let them hear their own voice; let them know what happens to any information and the tape and reassure them of confidentiality.

Questions

1 How long have you had an Independent Visitor? Have you had more than one Independent Visitor? If yes, explore.
2 Did you ask for an Independent Visitor or did someone suggest it? How did you find out about Independent Visitors/who suggested it?
3 Did you ask for a particular kind of person to be your Independent Visitor? e.g. young/older person; black/white; male/female. If yes, did you get the sort of person you wanted?
4 Did someone explain what the Independent Visitor does? If yes, who?
5 How often do you see your Independent Visitor? (use name)
6 Does s/he visit you at home? Do you go out?
7 What sort of things do you do with your Independent Visitor?
8 Does your Independent Visitor (use name) help you? If yes, how?
9 Can you talk to your Independent Visitor (use name) about any problems you may have? If yes, have they helped you with any of these problems? If no, is there someone else you can talk to? Who?

   or use scenario, e.g.

   If you were having difficulties at school, who would you talk to?
   If you were very unhappy about where you were living, who would you talk to?
   If you wanted to make a complaint about something, who would you ask to help you?
10 Has your Independent Visitor gone to any meetings with you? (e.g. review, school, medical/hospital, physio/occupational therapy). If yes, was this helpful? How was it helpful? If no, would you like your Independent Visitor to go to meetings with you?

11 Are there any other things you would like your Independent Visitor to do with you? If yes, what things?

12 What do you like about having an Independent Visitor?

13 What don't you like about having an Independent Visitor?

14 Do you think other children/young people should have an Independent Visitor? Why?

15 Are you happy with your Independent Visitor? If no, have you asked to change him/her?

16 Is there anything else you want to say about having an Independent Visitor?

Thank the child/young person for their help. Reassure them once again about confidentiality and what will happen to the information. A card or letter will be sent thanking them for their contribution.

Note The above list of questions are for guidance only, given the different ages and degrees of disability, i.e. some children/young people will be physically disabled whereas others will be learning disabled. The questions may need to be shortened, simplified or, if necessary, missed out altogether, and in some cases more scenario type questions may be used.

It will be important to collate the following information about the child/young person:

    age
    gender
    ethnicity
    disability
    type of placement
    length of time looked after by local authority
    circumstances around being referred for an Independent Visitor.

Appendix C
Questionnaire for interview with Independent Visitors

Warm up

Introductions; general chat; explain research project; thank them for agreeing to be involved; explain about how information will eventually be presented; reassure them of confidentiality; explain purpose of tape recorder and ask their permission to use it.

Questions

1 How long have you been an Independent Visitor?
2 How did you learn about Independent Visitors and what made you apply?
3 How were you assessed and approved?
4 What sort of training did you/do you get? Is this sufficient for the work?
5 What sort of support do you get? Is this adequate?
6 Do you get any specific training/support for visiting a disabled child/ young person? If yes, what? If no, do you think you should?
7 Did you request being matched with a disabled child/young person?
8 How long have you known _____? (child/young person)
9 How often do you visit _____?
10 What do you normally do together?
11 What, in your view, should Independent Visitors do?
12 Are there any ways in which the role could be clarified or improved?
13 What helps you in the role?
14 What hinders you in the role? Any problems with the role?
15 Are you doing what you expected when you applied to be an Independent Visitor?
16 Is it better/worse/just as you imagined?
17 Do you think the role differs if you are matched with a disabled child/ young person?
18 If you felt that the young person you are visiting needed something, such as more privacy, more choice over what they did or wore, what would you do?
19 Do you feel you've been able to help _____? (child/young person) In which ways?
20 Do you attend meetings with the young person? If yes, which ones? What do you do/say? If no, why not? Do you think you should?
21 Do you think you'll continue in the role? Yes or no, why?
22 Is there anything else you would like to say about being an Independent Visitor?

Thank person for taking part.

Note These questions are for guidance only as the interviews will be semi-structured. Collate information about the Independent Visitor, i.e. approximate age, gender, ethnicity, employment.

Appendix D
Questionnaire for interviews with Child's Foster Carer/ Residential Worker/Social Worker

Warm up

Introductions; general chat; explain research; thank them for agreeing to take part; explain how information will eventually be presented; reassure them of confidentiality; explain purpose of tape recorder and ask their permission to use it.

Questions

1 How long have you known _____? (child/young person)
2 Who suggested that _____ had an Independent Visitor? For what reasons? What did you think of the suggestion?
3 What were your initial reactions to _____ having an Independent Visitor? What do you feel about it now?
4 How often does the Independent Visitor visit?
5 Does _____ (child/young person) look forward to the visits? If yes, how do you know? Does s/he say? What signs are there?
6 What does _____ and the Independent Visitor usually do? Do they go out?
7 Does _____ and the Independent Visitor get on well together? Explore relationship.
8 What role do you think the Independent Visitor plays? What do you think of this role? (prompt: advantages/disadvantages/problems?)
9 Do you think the Independent Visitor has helped _____ in any way? If yes, how?
10 Has the Independent Visitor attended any meetings (e.g. review meeting) with _____? If yes, what do you think of this?
11 Do you think changes should be made to the role of the Independent Visitor?
12 Is there anything else you would like to say about being an Independent Visitor (e.g. his/her role, his/her relationship with _____)?

Thank the person for taking part.

Record status/relationship to young person of interviewee, i.e. foster carer/keyworker etc., so that this can be used as part of analysis.

Note These questions are for guidance only. The detail and order of the questions may change depending on the interviewee and the information obtained from the young person. This interview will be more detailed if a young person is not able to answer many of the questions in his or her interview. In writing up, it will need to be made clear that these answers are *not* the young person's.

Appendix E
Information sheets

Hello !!

I'm Abigail !!

I would like to talk to you at your foster or residential home about what it is like to have an Independent Visitor and how she or he helps you.

Your Independent Visitor, foster carer or keyworker will talk to you about this and see if you'll let me see you.

If this is OK, I'll come and visit you. Remember you can say whatever you want, because what you say is important and will help other children and young people get help from an Independent Visitor.

Please say Yes!! to talking to me – Your views count !!

Thanks!!!

Are you an Independent Visitor for a Child or Young Person who has a Disability?

Would you like to help raise the profile of Independent Visitors and how they can help disabled children and young people?

Please read on!

Abigail Knight is an independent social researcher and has been funded by the Joseph Rowntree Foundation, and supported by the National Institute for Social Work, to carry out a piece of research entitled: 'Valued or Forgotten: Independent Visitors and Disabled Children'. This is a new study and will examine how Independent Visitors are helping children and young people who have a physical or learning disability.

Abigail plans to talk to a total of 20 disabled children or young people, their Independent Visitor and one other person, such as their foster carer, residential worker or social worker. Where the young person has a severe disability which makes communication difficult, she would like to spend some time with the young person and Independent Visitor and perhaps be at the foster or residential home when the Independent Visitor arrives and/or leaves.

As an Independent Visitor for a young person with a disability, Abigail would like to talk to you about a number of issues, including:

* what it is like to be an Independent Visitor;
* what sort of training and support you receive;
* whether there are ways in which you've been able to help the young person;
* whether you think there are changes that should be made to the role.

She is happy to talk to you wherever you prefer, whether this is at your home or a neutral venue, and of course will see you whenever is most convenient, including weekends and evenings. The length of the meeting will depend on you and how much you want to say, but is likely to last for no more than an hour.

Please remember that whatever you say will be in complete confidence, and when the results are written up no names or places will be used to identify anyone.

You will be contacted for your help via the Independent Visitor Scheme Coordinator or by Abigail Knight, sometime in January, February or March 1997. You will not be contacted directly by Abigail Knight if you do not wish to take part.

Please help if you can. Many thanks!

Are you a Foster Carer or Keyworker for a Child or Young Person who has an Independent Visitor?

Would you like to help raise the profile of Independent Visitors and how they can help disabled children and young people?

Please read on!

Abigail Knight is a freelance social researcher and has been funded by the Joseph Rowntree Foundation, and supported by the National Institute for Social Work, to carry out a piece of research entitled: 'Valued or Forgotten: Independent Visitors and Disabled Children'. This is a new study and will examine how Independent Visitors are helping children and young people who have a physical or learning disability.

Abigail plans to talk to a total of 20 disabled children or young people, their Independent Visitor and one other person, such as their foster carer, residential worker or social worker. Where the young person has a severe disability which makes communication difficult, she would like to spend some time with the young person and Independent Visitor and perhaps be at the foster or residential home when the Independent Visitor arrives and/or leaves.

As a foster carer or keyworker for a young person with an Independent Visitor, Abigail would like to talk to you about a number of issues, including:

- what do you feel about the young person having an Independent Visitor;
- does the young person, in your view, look forward to the visits;
- whether there are ways in which the young person has been helped by the Independent Visitor;
- what you think of the role of the Independent Visitor.

She is happy to talk to you wherever you prefer, whether this is at your home, or a neutral venue, and of course will see you whenever is most convenient, including weekends and evenings. The length of the meeting will depend on you and how much you want to say, but is likely to last for no more than an hour.

Please remember that whatever you say will be in complete confidence, and when the results are written up no names or places will be used to identify anyone.

You will be contacted for your help via the Independent Visitor Scheme Coordinator, the Independent Visitor or by Abigail Knight sometime in January, February or March 1997.

Please help if you can. Many thanks!

References

Alderson, P (1995) *Listening to Children – Children, Ethics and Social Research.* Barnardo's

Alderson, P and Goodey, C (1996) 'Research with disabled children: how useful is child-centred ethics?', *Children and Society*, 10, 2

Baxter, C and others (1990) *Double Discrimination.* King's Fund Centre/Commission for Racial Equality

Beresford, B (1997) *Personal Accounts: Involving Disabled Children in Research.* HMSO

Brindle, D (1997) 'Labour wants "guardian angels" to end children's homes abuse', *Guardian*, 17 March

Cloke, C and Davies, M (1995) *Participation and Empowerment in Child Protection.* Pearsons Professional Limited, Pitman Publishing

Dalrymple, J and Hough, J eds (1995) *Having a Voice – An Exploration of Children's Rights and Advocacy.* British Association of Social Workers, Venture Press

Department of Health (1989) *Children Act 1989.* HMSO

Department of Health (1991) *The Children Act Guidance and Regulations: Volume 3 Family Placements and Volume 4 Residential Care.* HMSO

Department of Health (1996) *Statistical Bulletin 1996/8: Children Looked After by Local Authorities, Year Ending 31 March 1995.* HMSO

Franklin, B ed. (1995) *The Handbook of Children's Rights: Comparative Policy and Practice.* Routledge

Hamilton, C (1996) 'Rights not Rhetoric', *Community Care*, 26 September

HMSO (1992) *Capitalising on the Act – A Working Party Report on the Children Act 1989 in London.* HMSO

Hoodless, E (1997) 'Voluntary Movement', *Community Care*, 27 February

Hough, J (1995) 'Why isn't it the Children's Act?' *in* Dalrymple, J and Hough, J eds *Having a Voice.* British Association of Social Workers, Venture Press

Loughran, F, Parker, R and Gordon, D (1992) *Children with Disabilitites in Communal Establishments: A Further Analysis and Interpretation of the Office of Population Censuses and Surveys' Investigation.* University of Bristol

Marchant, R and Page, M (1993) *Bridging the Gap: Child Protection Work with Children with Multiple Disabilities*. NSPCC

Morris, J (1995) *Gone Missing? A Research and Policy Review of Disabled Children Living Away from their Families*. Who Cares? Trust

The National Centre for Volunteering (1996) *Involving Volunteers from Underrepresented Groups*. 'Findings' from the Joseph Rowntree Foundation

Poonia, K and Ward, L (1990) 'Fair Share of (the) Care?', *Community Care*, 11 January

Renvoize, J (1993) *Innocence Destroyed – A Study of Child Sexual Abuse*. Routledge

Rickford, F (1996) 'Fear of prejudice', *Guardian, 27 November*

Russell, P (1995) *Positive Choices – Services for Children with Disabilities Living Away from Home*. National Children's Bureau

Simons, K (1993) *Citizen Advocacy: The Inside View*. Joseph Rowntree Foundation/Norah Fry Research Centre

Social Services Inspectorate (1994) *Services to Disabled Children and their Families*. Department of Health

Swales, M (1992) 'Chemistry lessons', *Community Care*, 5 November

Swales, M (1993) 'Independent Visitors for children', *Children Act News*, October

Utting, Sir W (1991) *Children in the Public Care – A Review of Residential Child Care*. SSI, HMSO

Ward, L (1997) *Seen and Heard – Involving Children and Young People in Research and Development Projects*. York Publishing

Westcott, H (1993) *The Abuse of Children and Adults with Disabilities*. NSPCC

Index